Retailing in Salons & Spas

Revolutionize your Retailing Experience…
Boost Revenue & Profits!

Gerard Assey

Retailing in Salons & Spas

By

Gerard Assey

Publishing Agency:

Collection Skills

19/18, Palli Arasan Street

Anna Nagar East

Chennai - 600 102

ISBN: 978-93-92492-62-4

(Image by master1305 on https://www.freepik.com- Thank You)

Contents

Preface

Retail for you as an owner of a salon or spa is a huge potential to boost sales and increase revenues. You not only get to pick the items that will be displayed on your shelves, but you also get to keep all of the revenue- And it's not just about the money, either!

Providing take-home products for your clients is all about taking care of your clients' requirements. When clients leave your spa/ salon with a product in hand, you have made sure that they continue with the relaxing and uplifting experience they've just enjoyed. Sending your clients home with the items they will require to continue the treatment, feeling and looks, promotes customer retention and ensures client loyalty, according to research.

Studies indicate that 9 out of 10 people that leave a salon wished they had more education on how to recreate their new look. Further studies indicate that 71 percent of consumers were not given a product recommendation on a recent salon visit. A high-performing salon often retails its products to only 10% to 15% of its clients, and the reason the number is so low is because most therapists/ beauticians/ stylists don't even talk about products they use on their clients. Remember that until you demonstrate and explain what you're doing while using a product to a client, they will have no idea what you're doing. When you don't suggest retail to your consumer, you're actually giving them a bad experience. Customers want to appear amazing every day until their next visit, not just for one special day, in front of you. We all realize that people pay for much more than a treatment or good look; and these days what they really want is escapism as well as gorgeous results for as long as possible, and the opportunity and feeling to recreate those same looks and feelings at home can be priceless.

The client's pleasure, satisfaction, retention, future business and referrals are therefore directly impacted by the client's capacity to duplicate and continue with the same look and feeling at home. It all comes down to determining what your client needs are and providing a solution to fit it. When customers fall in love with the product you've recommended, they won't just come back to you to make another buy; they'll also trust your taste and recommendations for all future dealings, and become your advocates on your behalf- recommending others to you.

For this the spa/ salon staff should be trained to know the products well and be able to not only recommend the best solution, but also educate guests about the product's benefits and suitability for their individual needs and concerns. The focus shouldn't be on sales, but on SOLUTIONS!

Retailing should therefore never be looked at lightly or treated as a separate part of your business, but must be an integral part of everything you do in your spa/ salon- for this is another great avenue that generates substantial revenues. And if you don't; someone else will- thereby winning over your customers.

This book: **'Retailing in Salons & Spas'** is therefore a must have for anyone in the spa/ beauty salon/ health club and similar businesses to help you *'Revolutionize your Retailing Experience…and Boost Revenue & Profits!*

It covers in detail, key steps required for the Retail Sales and Customer Service Process- and is aimed at all spa/ salon owners, therapists, stylists, beauticians, receptionists, retail sales, customer service and shop floor staff, supervisors/team leaders and managers, who are keen on creating a memorable experience that is enjoyable by encouraging customers to return in the future!

The Big Plus with Retail is that, retail will never miss an appointment, nor leave you for another salon, or phone in sick. Retail can be that much dependable factor that moves your salon/spa business from a loss to a profit.

Just think for a Moment: *Potential profits could be walking out of the door every single day! Can your salon/ spa business afford this to be happening?*

Increase Sales in Your Spa/ Salon Today!

(*Not to us, O LORD, not to us, But to Your name give glory-* **Ps 115.1**)

Praises, Raves & Reviews

Here's what a sample of our Participants have to say after attending our sessions on:

'Professional Selling Skills for Spa's, Salons and Health Clubs'

&

Retail in Detail for Spa's, Salons & Health Clubs

"Very interesting....One of the best I have had in my life. After the training, I was clear about the objectives of selling in my spa....."

"It built our creativity & work in teams with open minds...Learnt a lot on up-selling, handling complaints politely & how to translate to profits! Awesome, Interesting!"

"Interesting & very useful information....the way to handle my Guests...very useful for my future...."

"I liked the fact that the Trainer was able to keep the attention & interest of the participants at ALL times...A lot of useful information...very informative!!! Forced us to think by ourselves"

"Excellent Training!"

"Clear, great information-loved the exercises, examples...I gained enough & valuable information-Gerard, A great Trainer!!!"

"Helped me greatly on my self-confidence, handling complaints & being customer focused!"

"Every part clearly understood...Gained extensive knowledge in selling, up-selling & cross-selling our services...Changed my personal attitude!!! Thanks a lot..."

Why is Retail Important for your Salon/ Spa?
What are the KEY Benefits?

Retailing products in your salon/spa can make a huge difference in the overall bottom line of your business, with the ability to drive customer loyalty perhaps being one of its biggest advantages. Here are some key benefits of Retailing:

- ✓ Improves Revenue per Client: The most obvious reason spa/ salon retailing benefits you is the increase in revenue. Retailing products in your salon/ spa helps generate more revenue from every client that visits your salon. It's widely accepted within the spa industry that spa/ salon retail sales should at least contribute to around 25 to 30 % of the organization's overall revenue
- ✓ Helps with the overall Profitability of the Business: Because the margins are usually higher with spa retail products, this is probably one of the foremost benefits from spa retail sales, contributing to the spa's overall profitability much more than many spa treatments.
- ✓ Enhances client loyalty and retention: When a client finds a beautician/ therapist that they trust, they'll stick with them for life. Not only do they leave your salon with an amazing feeling and looks, but you've demonstrated and helped them with the products to maintain that feeling and look. For instance, if you inform a client that you noticed that her hair is

appearing thinner when doing their hair, and you suggest a conditioner that will give her hair more volume- adding value to the customer's experience. Because you demonstrated that you genuinely care about your client and her hair, the likelihood that she would visit your salon again has just increased by 30%. Beauticians/ Therapists that demonstrate care have the customer's trust. A loyal customer will do more for your business in terms of advertising your business to other people who will, in turn, become your clients. They become your advocates, fighting out in the market on your behalf.

- ✓ Client base grows: Added to the above point, your revenue per client will also increase as your client base grows, which will help prove effective for keeping your business healthy and stable even in down times and both the short-term and long-term.
- ✓ Lasting treatment for the client: Maintaining the style and the beauty of the client's body or hair can be difficult for most lay people who have know no knowledge of hair styling or spas, and because of which many people lose their lovely hairstyles or that feeling almost immediately when they leave your salon/ spa. But if you sold them the right hair/ body care products that will help them to maintain that feeling and beauty, then what you get is a happy customer who would always choose your salon/spa over another. Retailing can really extend a client's journey beyond the physical environment of your salon/ spa where

they get to experience the same treatments at home with your products.

- ✓ It demonstrates that the staffs are knowledgeable: Knowledge is power, and demonstrating that you are an authority on your products makes you someone who should be taken seriously. Therefore, it is important to understand the advantages of each of your items so that you can explain these to customers and why they are the greatest choice for them. Customers will naturally pay attention to you and your experienced employees, thus improving the likelihood of a profitable retail transaction.
- ✓ More Money with Less Talking: You get to make more money with less talking as the probability for repeat sales to the same client, and referral purchases are high- and you don't have to put in much effort now.
- ✓ It boosts your salon reputation: Many people avoid selling for fear of being seen as pushy. However, if done correctly, (and that's what this book will help you do) sales can actually improve your salon reputation.
- ✓ Retailing to clients can help build trust: Retailing to customers can assist establish trust because they are more inclined to heed staff advice as they already have some level of confidence in the beauticians and therapists that are treating them. Staff members can increase customer trust and loyalty by recommending the most appropriate products for a post-treatment routine that are advised to individuals booked onto specific treatments.

- ✓ Some other benefits of retailing treatments and products to the client are: professional image and ethics, improved aftercare and homecare advice, and an ever growing list of happy customers seeing and feeling the benefits that will help promote the spa/ salon and return for more thus increasing profits.

Benefits for salon/ spa professionals

- ✓ The salon/ spa professional is benefitted in a number of ways including increased salary/ commissions and/or other rewards and recognitions.
- ✓ A supplementary benefit from spa retailing could also be a more than satisfying job experience and employability.
- ✓ More opportunities to receive free or discounted spa retail products, and the possibility to earn rewards from recognition programs and awards such as "Most Productive Employee/Retailer of the month" and similar contests.
- ✓ Opportunities to demonstrate care and leadership, thus opening chances for movement upwards

Creating a Retailing Culture

It starts with the right culture. If you are looking at being successful at Retailing in your Salon/ Spa, then your topmost priority must be to set the right culture within. Just placing retail items on the spas/ salon's tables or shelves won't encourage consumers to make purchases. No one will give it a second glance if you just do this alone. But if you are really keen on selling your retail products (and you must be-as it is a massive revenue generator!), you must first develop a retail culture all throughout your facility.

The expectation that is set and continuously promoted within the salon towards retail sales is what will bring the desired results. So here are some key areas that you can look at to build in this culture:

1. It begins by having a strong leader who will inspire and drive the beauticians and therapists and hold them continuously responsible to the standards that they must follow. Strong, consistent leadership from a staff member with retail credibility can help.
2. Identify what are your Differentiators? What distinguishes your salon/ spa? An essential component of your brand is the culture. This distinguishes your salon/ spa from others. So when it comes to retailing, work on arranging the items/ products in accordance with your spa/salon's culture. Study the other Spa's/ Salon's with the same objective as yours, and make necessary alterations in order to maintain your differences. But whatever you do, do not attempt to sell goods that you or

your customers find objectionable or dislike. Never neglect to always keep researching competitors' strategies to look at various ways to stay ahead.

3. Set Your Retail Goals: It is vital to let everyone in your salon/ spa know what is expected of them- and this is done as soon as they are hired. They should be made aware of everything by having it written out properly and signed.
4. Set weekly sales targets: Decide on the targets and keep a running scoreboard or tab on the progress.
5. Display the Objectives prominently: Your spas/ salon's retail objectives should be prominently visible to everyone. Remember if you cannot see the target, you cannot hit it. Each employee's performance must be displayed, with them updating their own statistics each day in either red or black, depending on how well they are doing in comparison to the targets. This board can be used for your weekly or monthly contests or other methods for rewarding performances with fun, motivating retail contests and good prizes worthy of the effort.
6. Set Appropriate Standards and it starts from the Top: The retail manager or person in-charge of retail must set the standard within the salon/ spa by ensuring that everyone addresses retailing solutions with EVERY CLIENT without getting slack. Consistency is the key.
7. Build and Maintain the Culture: It takes ongoing work to maintain the ideal culture

once everyone is fully aware of what is expected of them- and unless someone actively, continuously and constantly influences them through strong leadership, beauticians/ therapists won't change on their own. You achieve this by demonstrating great leadership, encouraging teamwork, and inspiring pride in their role to the spa's/ salon's success.

8. Keep your staffs' attention and focus on retail: Even if you build the ideal retail atmosphere, you will still lose sales if your beauticians and therapists are not on board. Customers who make product purchases are more loyal and feel a connection to the salon, and it's the beauticians and therapists that are actually the ones who make these connections, by getting the correct items and information into the hands and minds, which ultimately aids in retaining them.
9. Educate and Train staff on your products: Constant training on new products, its applications and benefits must be covered regularly. Here are some ways to do so:

✓ Arrange for beauty product manufacturer's educators to come to your spa/ salon and provide product knowledge training on their products.

✓ The Retail Manager must also conduct regular contests, quizzes and questions to test product knowledge.

✓ Have each member of your staff do some research on one product of a line and present sales benefits in every meeting.

- ✓ Practice Makes Sales: If you're still uneasy about selling, we advise starting by attempting to persuade a colleague or another beautician or therapist in your facility to buy a product. Try having them raise a couple of objections that customers would actually bring up, so you will be able to gain confidence and be more professional when handling real customers
- ✓ Make use of product flashcards! The greatest approach to educating oneself is to test your knowledge, in addition to just utilizing the product. Try to recall interesting details about every product you sell. The more knowledgeable you are about your products, the more equipped you are to offer advice based on the wants and concerns of customers. Develop flash cards for each product that you can effectively use when explaining to customers

10. You must have a detailed Plan of Action

- ✓ Who will lead this retail sales effort? (Someone with proven credibility- strong leadership that will hold others accountable)
- ✓ What are the products you have for retailing?
- ✓ Can you tie up with some manufacturers/ distributors- to have special products featured each week?
- ✓ When are you planning to start and roll out this without any looking back?
- ✓ What can you do to educate the team on say a product line each week/ month?
- ✓ What type of contest/ incentives/ commissions are you planning to offer for the targets worked on?

- ✓ What sort of prizes you think the team would run for?
- ✓ What type of promotional material you will need to promote your campaigns externally to customers and internally to your team? (Posters/ Mailers/ Social media etc)

The G.R.E.A.T. Sales Model
Importance of this 5 Step Process

Only now we are actually getting into the Selling Process…so before we go any further, let us ask ourselves: What is selling? What comes to your mind when you hear the word 'Selling' or 'Sale'?

I can guarantee you that for most people, the very first words that pop up into our minds would be words like *'revenue, profits, quotas, targets, etc'*…all related to money! Shouldn't this then only confirm what came up in a survey that was conducted on reasons of what customers 'hate about sales people'? Most times, sales people are more concerned with what is in the customers' wallet, his check book or the business that she brings, than genuinely helping the customer.

But if we could change that thinking to a feeling that selling is more of *'Need Solving/ Concern Handling'*, it would then change our entire perspective of the selling process and the way we treat the customer particularly. Let us now change that hat that we have been wearing from a sales person to that of a 'Consultant or Advisor'! Someone has a problem, concern or need some help and have walked into your salon/outlet - your job is to genuinely help that person get out of that situation, then only will your whole perception towards the selling process change.

It is like what happens when a patient visits a doctor. A genuine doctor, will never prescribe, until he has really diagnosed the problem completely. When this happens the customers' confidence and respect for the expert treating her zooms up. She now begins to trust you a professional expert, thus leading to rapport and a lasting relationship

Whatever be the Profession…Everyone Sells!

As a Baby, as a Wife, as a Daughter/Son, as an Employer, as an Employee…As a Beautician or Therapist…You are always selling!

Everything runs on this profession- company, economies, countries!

So what are you really selling? Dreams, beauty, gorgeous looks, health, relaxation, de-stress, feeling and looking younger or much more?

Health: *To support your clients journeys to better wellness.*

Beauty: *To support your clients journeys to looking and feeling younger and even more beautiful*

You are therefore in the business of changing lives with your HEART, HEAD and HANDS!!!

When it comes to your business in particular, you are selling 4 areas:

- ✓ Yourselves *(Customers go by what they see in you first- the way you carry and conduct yourself- already covered in an earlier chapter)*
- ✓ Your Services
- ✓ Retailing your Products
- ✓ The Salon Image…

If you look at the word 'SALE' – the word actually tells you in an acronym the steps that one should follow. Most times, a person, just rushes into providing his pitch on the product or service, without actually taking time to understand the specific need of a customer. This acronym should be a reminder for us to

STOP (think!)
Ask Questions (to understand the specific need of the customer),
Listen to understand…and finally
Engage, Enthuse & Excite the customer, by letting the customer do more of the talking

The Foundation of the Sales Process

Haven't you noticed that when a good therapist/ beautician leaves an organization and her regular clients get to know of it, most of them want to know where she has joined? What do you think could be the reason that makes someone buy/ deal only with a particular company, beautician or therapist?

You will be surprised to note that most times, the reason is neither the product, nor the price, but rather the **relationship** with the person with whom they're dealing. Products will change, services will change, prices will change, economies and market places will change too– but if the relationship is strong, the account endures. And I have seen many accounts move as the beautician/ therapist or other professional person moved from the company too.

The only thing that truly matters is the relationship between the seller and the buyer.

When you don't have an edge in product technology or price, then you need an edge in the way you connect with people.

And the foundation of relationship is an important word: TRUST. To make a buying decision, a customer has to make a leap of faith. Customers will not buy from a person they don't trust, don't like, or someone that doesn't show confidence. Successful professionals create a safety net called trust. Trust helps your customers take that leap in complete confidence.

How to Build Trust?

Trust is confidence born of 3 dimensions:
Character, Credibility and Competence

- ✓ Character includes your integrity, motive, and intent with people.
- ✓ Competence includes your capabilities, skills, abilities, results, and track record. Both dimensions are vital.
- ✓ However, the foundation of trust is your own Credibility, and it can be a real differentiator. When a therapist/ beautician's credibility and reputation is high, it enables the person to establish trust fast – and for life.

Here are some things you can do to improve your trust with clients.

- ✓ Never lie
- ✓ Value your clients' time
- ✓ Never break a promise
- ✓ Listen more-talk less
- ✓ Offer services/ products that are tailored to their needs
- ✓ Demonstrate you are knowledgeable
- ✓ Provide professional advice
- ✓ Communicate at every stage
- ✓ Be transparent about your work process
- ✓ Avoid your personal opinions/ agenda
- ✓ Stay in touch
- ✓ Remain ethical in all dealings

When it comes to selling services or products, many personnel in spa's, salons or health clubs do not follow a structured process, especially when it comes to retailing their products-but usually prefer to allow the sale to flow without control- it is like taking a shot in the dark, which can put them in a fix or result in loss of much of potential business opportunities.

The G.R.E.A.T Sales Model can save you from all of this. Unlike the traditional hard sell approach where you are constantly 'pushing' the customer to close right from the start- thus making the customer feel uncomfortable, manipulated or threatened, with this G.R.E.A.T. Sales Model, the person takes time up front to build a sincere, committed relationship by investing time in learning about the customer's needs and knowing when to start retailing. This helps build trust between the two. Then, every step of the process that follows is conducted with the relationship in mind, ensuring an enduring and lasting relationship, leading to repeat business and referrals. The G.R.E.A.T. Sales Model helps you in many ways:

- ✓ It first of all reminds you that only great service stands out
- ✓ It gives you a structured approach to handling your customers which is an acronym for a 5 step sales model and process.

These 5 steps are the key to successful selling, especially for retailing when you have a good range

G-Greet the Customer

R-Revealing Questions-Understanding their Needs

E-Explain, Enlighten, Engage, Enthuse, Excite Customers about your Product

A-Answer Customer's Concerns and Objections

T-Techniques to help your customer 'buy'…'*as people, hate being sold*!

-Selling to the opposite sex

-Generating Additional Sales

-Suggesting Complementary/ Add-on Products/ Up-Selling/ Cross-Selling

-Thank them

With the GREAT Sales Model, most of your time is 'invested' in uncovering the customer's needs and proving value of your services and products, before you actually recommend it, thus eliminating many objections later on. It is designed to make you more structured and professional in your approach and ensure that your customer feels 'important' by focusing on the customer rather than on the sale!

Most personnel concentrate on the close, but the key is to concentrate and stay focused on the process rather than on the outcome or close. From our experience of conducting several workshops, over these last 22 years (as of Mar 2023), we have noticed that where personnel have made a dedicated and conscious effort to apply these key steps of the GREAT Model- they have found tremendous results in their productivity, confidence and sales revenues. So work through each step instead of trying to close the sale and you will start to see better results along with being more confident and professional on your job.

Here are some things that can make a difference between Professional/ Consultative Selling and a Hard Selling (Pushy) approach.

Professional Selling:

- ✓ Uses the client's name
- ✓ Thorough knowledge of the products and services available
- ✓ Keen listener, asks appropriate questions, and shows genuine interest
- ✓ Identifies needs, and helps clients make decisions

- ✓ Highlights the benefits and value of services and products
- ✓ Empathizes (putting yourself in the client's shoes)
- ✓ Recognizes body language
- ✓ Highly enthusiastic
- ✓ Congratulates client on their purchase, e.g. '*You've made an excellent choice – I'm most certain you will find that it works well for you'*

Hard Selling (Pushy)

- ✓ Interrupts the client
- ✓ Floods clients with theory and science
- ✓ Argues and wants to have own way by telling the client that they are wrong
- ✓ Very pushy
- ✓ Threatens the client, e.g *'It will go up in price next week'*
- ✓ Insists and manipulates the client to buy the product

The GREAT Sales and Service Professional Prepares!

Before we get into each of the 5 key steps of the GREAT Sales Model, I believe there is yet another important step that can help you stand out from the rest, as a true Professional, and that is to be prepared. It can as such, be likened to the basic foundation of a call. Preparation is vital, as it provides the research and base required to pursue an intelligent and productive customer experience.
Before we go any further into this, let us first ask: Why Prepare?

- ✓ *It makes you feel more confident*
- ✓ *You are able to discuss intelligently*
- ✓ *Saves time- yours and the customers*
- ✓ *You get to understand the customer's potential needs better*
- ✓ *You become more aware of the business*
- ✓ *Helps you study and understand the competition*
- ✓ *Enables you know the markets, industry and environment*
- ✓ *Your customers respect for you goes up*
- ✓ *You are looked as a professional in the eyes of the customer*
- ✓ *Customer knows you are there to help- not extract*
- ✓ *You are proving that you are unlike other personnel in other set-ups*

A person has no right to service a customer if she isn't prepared to do so. On the other hand, when a customer sees a professional as being prepared, her respect for the person and the company that she represents zooms up. There is instant trust, bonding and rapport

How fair is it to a customer when a so called professional tries to solicit business that is worth several thousands of money, without doing any groundwork of being prepared? When a customer is going to part with several thousands of her money, shouldn't you as a professional do some amount of ground work, so you are well prepared to service them better?. This is what will lead to respect, resulting in enhanced credibility and a lifelong relationship, because now the customer can see clearly that you, as a professional is genuinely interested in helping her, and not just after her money!

A lot of people think that selling has a lot to do with 'being lucky'! My answer is that 'Good Selling' is not a 'matter of Luck', but rather a combination of Preparation plus Opportunity where Preparation accounts for 99%. Now when 99% of efforts have been put in, and that 1% opportunity gets by you, then that is what will make you the so called 'lucky person'

But if you are unprepared and that 1% opportunity comes by, it will just go past you and move to some other outlet that is more prepared to welcome such an opportunity.

Preparation is therefore, without a doubt, the key to a successful business opportunity. Very often we hear customers say: "I'll come back!" but sadly, many never do. Why?

- ✓ *The receptionist did not greet and acknowledge the customer properly.*

- ✓ *The therapist wasted a lot of time setting herself up in front of the customer and did not know where the items were in the outlet*
- ✓ *The therapist did not have sufficient knowledge of the product / how it worked and what would be the benefits of using the same*
- ✓ *The therapist/ beautician did not ask the customer the right questions to uncover the customer's specific need.*
- ✓ *The therapist delivered a rehearsed/ canned presentation during the so-called counseling session, instead of focusing on the customer's need*
- ✓ *The therapist rattled the technical features of the product instead of what the product would do for the customer*

We can go on and on! But as we can see, being thoroughly prepared is being an 'Eagle System Professional' and just as how an eagle is focused and watchful, an Eagle System Professional spends a good amount of her time on this part, as they prefer to 'prepare than repair' or have any regrets later.

Let's look at what to prepare:

Selling Yourself: Before you decide to sell anything, the customer must be sold on you first! Customers these days have high expectations in terms of client service and to be successful and stand out you must not only meet those needs and expectations but go beyond. And to effectively do this, you must be able to put yourself in your clients' shoes, as they are putting their trust in your hands, by believing in your ability- so you need to live up to it and make sure that they feel comfortable and safe.

This industry is highly competitive, so it is vital that you keep your skills and knowledge up to date to.

Your Personal Grooming

Mental/ Physical Grooming (Well groomed, clean and hygienic- from the top of your head to the tip of your toes- smelling good)

Your Store-Equipment, Gadgets and Products- be thorough

- ✓ Know your company
- ✓ Know all your services/ products: performance/ features/ benefits/pricing/ drawbacks
- ✓ Know the location of stocks/ placement of products-stock levels and where located
- ✓ Know your company's policies and systems
- ✓ Know how to handle various professional gadgets/ equipment, including billing machines, credit card machines etc.
- ✓ Know the various combinations/ mixes and the after-effects it has on an individual

Your Competitors

- ✓ Know as much details about your competitors thoroughly
- ✓ Who are the other players?
- ✓ Where does your organization stand in relation or comparison with them?
- ✓ What are their USP's etc?
- ✓ Have the comparison of features/ benefits with competitors ready at hand.
- ✓ How does your company's services or products compare with the competition- the strengths/ weaknesses etc?
- ✓ Besides the standard skin care, hair, body treatments, and massage therapies, is there

anything that makes them stand out from the crowd?

- ✓ Are there any services that you intend to offer that are not on your competitors' menu?
- ✓ What can you do to be different?
- ✓ What are your competitors charging for their services?

Never Bad-mouth your Competition!

While on this subject of preparing information about the competition, an important point to keep in mind here is that as a professional you must never badmouth a competitor's product line. Instead, find out what the client does or does not like about another product and use it as an opportunity to educate them on the difference in ingredients and benefits in products. For example if a client mentions that they are using a cleanser from another product line then give them a compliment: *"I am really so delighted that you understand the importance of proper skin care and are regularly cleansing it!"* If the customer goes into details about the line, and you are thorough on the differences, then subtly try to point out differences: *"One of the key differences in our line is that none of our cleansers contain mineral oil or artificial fragrance."* Do this without putting the other product down or getting into any comparisons

Your Market/ Industry

- ✓ Know the market/ industry you operate in thoroughly eg; Spas., health clubs, gymnasiums, beauty parlors/ salons/ hospitality in general,
- ✓ What is the market like?
- ✓ Do you know what are the trends/ regulations/ government policies about the industry you are in?

- ✓ Are you up to date with what is happening?

Your Sales Tools

- ✓ Advertising/ Promotional material/ Brochures/ Pricelists
- ✓ Gadgets/ Equipment- check their cleanliness/ working/ fully charged etc.
- ✓ Your name badge/ ID card
- ✓ Business cards
- ✓ Calculators
- ✓ Batteries/ Cells/ Chargers for demonstration of electronic products
- ✓ Copies of articles on products featured in newspapers /magazines
- ✓ Relevant industry news
- ✓ Loyalty membership forms/ procedures
- ✓ Samples/ demo pieces
- ✓ Customer endorsement letters /Testimonials from satisfied customers
- ✓ A List of satisfied customers
- ✓ A Referrals book
- ✓ Writing pad/ Pens that write

Selling the Salon/Spa Image

90% of lasting impressions are created in the first 90 seconds. Therefore the salon image and what is projected as a customer walks in, is vital, and all of this is the combined responsibility of the salon owner, supported by his/her staff.

- ✓ Clients see: colors, layout, cleanliness, staff appearance and attitude.
- ✓ Clients hear: telephone greetings, personal greetings on arrival, music, background noise.
- ✓ Clients smell: products, staff hygiene, coffee

Here are some aspects of the Physical Environment to watch for:

- ✓ The frontage, the signage's, the window displays- all need to arrest the customer's attention and attract the customer into your premises.
- ✓ Security
- ✓ Car parking facilities
- ✓ Ambience/ Spaciousness/ Aesthetics/ Lighting/ Room temperature
- ✓ Soft music (or music depending on the service/products sold)
- ✓ Comfort level/ reach of products
- ✓ Safe and comfortable for children
- ✓ Overall showroom cleanliness
- ✓ Toilets/ Washrooms cleanliness
- ✓ Ensuring the outlet is busy, with movement…even if it has to have some employees act like customers… As the best attraction is a busy outlet.

Linen, robes, shoes and towels are expected to be clean and free of odors and stains. The amenities must be impeccably clean, with attendants constantly circling the area to ensure all needs are met. There are standards that must be upheld—proper draping, product knowledge, timing, pricing quotes if upgrading, checking in about comfort and preferences, and maintaining a serene presence. Maybe a specific place for jewelry and phones, adjustable tables with heat, and music options for the guest. The rooms need to be spacious, quiet and beautifully decorated, containing everything, besides the essential tools, gadgets and equipments around, other things like even a warm neck roll, essential oils, lotions, scrubs, warm stones, and other supplies should be stocked ahead of time, that the therapist/beautician may need during a session. Also if the rest of the guest's schedule is known and kept ready to guide her into her next treatment or back to the lounge will greatly exhibit a professional and memorable touch.

I have a number of case studies and examples of how by not providing the right physical environment, customers or staff moved out, never to return. Here is an example that just popped into my mind:

True case study: I remember a consulting assignment that we undertook for a jeweler client. Everything was in place for a new beginning, with all hopes of the sales zooming up. Training provided to the team, showroom remodeled, uniforms provided, competitive prices and schemes, enough publicity...everything all set in anticipation.

After 3 months of all of this, sales seemed fairly low and not as expected. Obviously I was surprised for I was so sure and confident that there was going to be an upward trend like never before! The Managing Director was no doubt very disappointed after all those extra investments he had made, so he called me for a meeting to express this disappointment. I asked him to give me a couple of days to study the situation. I used this time to do a couple of things:

I set up a mystery customer (somebody who would act as a customer without anyone knowing). I got one of my staff members to note all his experiences right from the time he drove in. Now it must be noted here that this jeweler was located in one on the most prime localities in the city, with a number of other jewelers around too. Being a prime, market area, car parking was one of the major problems, and any showroom that had their own parking spaces had a major benefit and advantage. Fortunately, this particular jeweler had enough car parking spaces, for about 12 cars at a time.

As my mystery customer drove into the compound of this jeweler to park his vehicle, the security guard followed the car and approached this 'customer' telling him that the space was for the MD and the staff and that he would need to park elsewhere. At this point there were four parking slots already available. On trying to convince the guard that it would be a matter of few minutes that he would be back after a purchase, the guard stubbornly insisted that this 'customer' take his car and park it elsewhere. He finally drove out of the showroom and after about 25 minutes of circling the entire neighborhood, he managed to get a vacant spot under a tree near a roadside.

He had to walk another eight minutes or so to get to the showroom. Finally to make a long story short, his experience at every other stage from the time he entered to the time he exited was rated as excellent. So without a doubt we now had an indication of where the problem was. Our next step was to have this confirmed, so we had a survey form created with several factors listed and had a professional market research agency call all on most of the customers that they had listed on their database. Every item on the survey was ticked as excellent, but when it came to the area of parking and treatment by the security guard- you don't have to guess what the response was! A good 88% of the responses indicated the rude and harsh behavior of the security guard that resulted in customers moving elsewhere to shop. It was like directly telling customers to please go elsewhere- We do not want you! And remember, if someone else could treat them as royals, these customers are never going to come back to you!

When preparing it is a good idea to: Think of 4 Cs
Customer, **C**ompetitor, **C**apabilities, and **C**ost (Value)
Customer:

- ✓ *Do they know your organization? Are they frequent clients/ new to the store?*
- ✓ *What information do they have about your organization?*
- ✓ *What information do you have about them?*

Competitor:

- ✓ *Who are your Competitors?*
- ✓ *What are their positions in the eyes of the customer?*
- ✓ *How does the customer see/ perceive them?*
- ✓ *Brainstorm their strengths/weaknesses*
- ✓ *What aspects of the requirement which (from your knowledge of your competition) you can speculate your competitor will address more effectively than you.*

Capabilities:

- ✓ *What are your capabilities?*
- ✓ *Do you stand out from the competition? In what areas?*

Cost (Value)

- ✓ *What value are you bringing to the customer? How would she view it?*
- ✓ *What more could you consider doing to delight the customer?*

Before we actually get into the first step of the GREAT Sales Model, as part of your preparation, here are a few: **Do's and Don'ts when standing in the Customers Area**

- ✓ Stand erect, weight balanced on both feet. Do not lean against anything.
- ✓ Hands to be kept straight on your sides.
    - Not in pockets.
    - Not on the hips.
    - Not behind the back.
- ✓ Do not cross arms across the chest.
- ✓ Do not stand in groups and chat.
- ✓ Walk at an even pace, do not rush or run.
- ✓ Avoid making any sound or loud noise.
- ✓ Give customers the right of way and move aside for approaching customers.
- ✓ Do not point fingers or stare towards customers.
- ✓ Do not talk about the customer, even if not around with the customer (her ears are still open).
- ✓ Keep telephone conversations short and concise.
- ✓ Personal calls / mobiles should not be entertained on the floor.

Exercise!

- ✓ At the Outlet what are the Do's & Don'ts in terms of your behavior!
- ✓ How should your showroom/outlet be?
- ✓ What are the other issues to be considered-Displays, Valet, Signboards, Security etc
- ✓ What are some of the items you need to keep at hand?
- ✓ What could you do to give your customers a WOW experience!

So as can be seen, for you to be an effective Professional you will need to work on being organized and have **SYSTEM.S.** When you do have **SYSTEMS**, you will find that it will help…

Save
You
Stress
Time
Energy
Money and…
Sleepless Nights!
…While also enhancing your credibility and productivity!

Your Inventory and Displays

How you organize your inventory and display can help a lot in adding to more sales. So here some tried and tested tips to get going on this:

1. Allocate Space: As the very first step, you must determine how much space is being allocated- a prominent location- making it visually attractive. Try not to have a cluttered retail display-(ideally keep about six products at most- if at a station)
2. Less is more! Studies on consumer behavior have indicated that when individuals have too many options, they don't buy anything. So offer options, but not too many. Don't stock too many items. Create a series of tiny collections out of your products. Showcase various product categories according to their intended usage in clear groups. For instance, it would be confusing and time-consuming for someone looking at moisturizers or treatments to help with frizzy hair to go through a whole lot of other goods mixed in with them, before they really find what they need.
3. Categorize your Products: So the next step is to properly categorize your products and items by color, shape, or brand or use such as:
    - ✓ Styling products
    - ✓ Hair and Scalp Care
    - ✓ Shampoos
    - ✓ Conditioners
    - ✓ Skin/ Body Care and Cleansing
    - ✓ Nail and Cuticle Products
    - ✓ Oral Hygiene Products

- ✓ Candles & Fragrances
- ✓ Formulations- Balms, Creams, Gels, Oils etc
- ✓ Jewelry
- ✓ Makeup
- ✓ Equipment

4. Display Products at the Right Location: Your product displays must be well placed to stand out and get attention. Start by placing products in can't-miss locations where people's eyes naturally focus, like near the entrance, next to mirrors or better still in a waiting area, or next to the place where people sit. Stations cluttered with products will not help in enticing clients to buy.
5. Arrangement of Products: When entering a store, we most often move to the right. To encourage your customers to start spending, take advantage of this by positioning your retail specials and best-sellers on the right hand side.
6. Furthermore, according to studies, we scan product shelves from left to right, so organize your products in such a way that higher prices are to the right- the more expensive items on the right side of your display, the more likely it is that your customer will choose to purchase one of them.
7. Placement of Items: Remember that Eye-height is buy-height
8. Eye-level shelves are packed with the most profitable brands and premium items.
9. Budget and discount items are harder to spot on the lower shelves.

10. Impulse buys are placed between waist height and eye-level.
11. One great tip is to keep a selection of tempting impulse buys in a basket at reception – for example, travel-size skin care products during the vacation season or ready-wrapped last-minute items during Easter time.
12. Use Odd numbers when displaying: Display retail products in groups of three or five. This is because odd numbers are more appealing to the eye.
13. Use all your Windows: Use your window space effectively to display your retail product range. You can monitor and test each display arrangement, by keeping a record of what works well.
14. Ensure a Visual balance: Place items with darker color packaging lower down and light color packaging higher up- to prevent a 'top-heavy' look.
15. Brighten up the Display: Use accent lighting, or just colored light bulbs or series of sparkling lights to draw attention to product displays.
16. Keep changing your displays: People get bored, looking at the same things always, so make sure you change your spa/salon product displays on a regular basis. An ideal and good rule of thumb is on a monthly basis, when you can make simple changes to reflect for example seasons or special occasions such as: Christmas, Easter, New Year, summer holidays and special days such as Mother's/ Daughters Day. You might like to add any new products to your range that can freshen up and brighten the looks of your displays.

17. Use Disruptors: 'Disruptors'-like tables full of merchandise that customers must pass by or navigate to reach their beautician's or therapists station is a good approach to grab their attention. These "disrupters" can be successful selling venues for salon/ spa retail if you are deliberate about the items you place on them.
18. Use clear product signs – Self Talkers: These are little labels or signs that highlight the product name, price, size of the ingredients and benefits of the product. Usually people hate to ask about how much something costs and would rather leave empty-handed without finding out, so make sure your pricing is absolutely clear, stating any taxes if so. If you are having a sale on certain items, then a nice catchy sign on this shelf, next to the product-should indicate the same. And always have the product labels facing out toward your client.
19. Try having your products featured in front- as the first point, away from the receptionist, so this would enable walk-in customers to browse through the products before they talk to the receptionist.
20. Encourage browsing: Never hide your retail away in a glass cabinet or on shelves behind your reception. Encourage browsers with easily accessible open shelves to hold in their hands, try out or ask questions.
21. Make your retail area tempting. Having a small juice/ tea / coffee dispenser near the retail area is a great way to entice clients to move out of their chairs to your retail shelves (not

cupboards- as people usually do not like to reach into cupboards or cabinets).

22. Tempt with Complementary Items: Ensure that related products are placed next to each other on the shelf. This will help double or triple your sales by inspiring customers to purchase complementary goods. For instance, make sure your conditioners for oily hair are adjacent to your displays of shampoos for that type of hair, and put lipsticks next to lip pencils, and after-sun care next to sun protection etc
23. Music Helps: Research shows that people tend to buy more expensive items when classical music is playing so choose a playlist with a slow, soft beat- that can create the right ambience and mood.
24. Try producing an "arena effect" if the setting and design permit. When your customers are waiting, having the products all around them gives them the chance to look at them from every angle.
25. No space? No problem! If you only have one wall for retail, then try getting creative by making it stand out with a nice wall color or art that compliments the bottles or packaging. Or you could just have shelves that hang from the ceiling displaying a few products- this could indeed be eye- catching. Also, make sure your products are well lit – They must be able to see or read your products and shelf talkers
26. Offer Test Products: Encourage your customers to test products- you could do so by ensuring that they are between 22 and 66 inches; as these are proven heights for easy

accessibility. Also, try an inviting “try me!” or “test me out” label.

27. Offer retail guidance: Don’t leave your customers just looking at the product display and waiting for them to ask for more details. Talking them through what’s on offer and making recommendations is key. Have someone always nearby ready to help out
28. Keep your retail shelf organized, clean and dust-free: No one would want to buy a product that is dusty- not only is it visually unappealing, but it also looks like no one else liked or touched the product enough to buy it. So make sure your product display units and the products on them are kept pristine. Have a schedule and plan so they are thoroughly dusted and properly arranged say at least once a week.
29. Promote these Displays: Take pictures of your retail product displays regularly and publish them on Instagram, FB, your website and other social media to let your customers see your colorful displays and get excited about featured products.
30. Avoid Spoilage and Shrinkage: Most of the products will have a shelf life or expiry date, and not utilizing them or selling them before that date can be a loss of profit. This can include expired products, damaged products, and wastage. When inventory isn’t moving off of your shelf –it’s a loss of income. So you will need to keep a track of such products and have ways to move them through incentive schemes or offers before the expiry dates.

G- Greet the Customer

According to studies, people make up to 11 assumptions within the first 45 seconds of meeting someone for the first time, and these can include assumptions like their intelligence, level of success, education, knowledge, and expertise to name a few. This can sometimes be really dangerous- meaning that we only have one opportunity to make a great first impression. A smart professional- whether it is a receptionist, a therapist, beautician or whomever, will therefore grab this opportunity, as very rarely is there a second chance. If we fail to make a positive impact immediately, we will have to work harder to establish all that trust and credibility all over again.

And a smart professional can begin to display care and professionalism even before a customer walks in to the outlet with a few Important pre-arrival questions that can help a lot in:

- ✓ Safety: Asking a few basic health-related questions will help ensure that the treatment the client has chosen is appropriate and safe for them because many therapies are not safe or fit for everyone. Some of the services may be suitable due to conditions that the client could be going through; like heart disease, epilepsy, pregnancy, and powerful drugs like steroids. So always put your safety first!
- ✓ Customer service: When making a reservation, asking a few pertinent questions shows the customer you care about them and appreciate their business. Simple queries like whether they know how to get to the salon or

where to park, for instance, demonstrates consideration and begins to establish a rapport, helping you stand out from your competition.

- ✓ Client satisfaction: It might be challenging to control a customer's expectations when they arrive at your spa or salon if you don't know why they choose a specific service. Knowing what the patient is anticipating from the treatment they have scheduled might help avoid disappointment and clear up any confusion. In order to build a strong client relationship from the time of booking, pre-arrival inquiries can be helpful.
- ✓ Salon management: The right pre-arrival questions can help a lot to find a replacement right away if it turns out that a client pre-booked a treatment that is completely inappropriate for them when they arrive. This frequently leads to issues with reassigning rooms and furnishings and can give the salon a messy appearance. Pre-arrival queries make it easier for you to plan ahead and effectively use your resources.
- ✓ Maximising staff: Pre-arrival inquiries might also make it easier for you to manage your crew. Finding a different course of treatment quickly might require finding a different team to provide it.

A customer's impressions are influenced by our setup, clothes, how we look, behave and the way we speak.

What do customers see in the first 30 seconds?

- ✓ Smile: Pleasant and genuine.

- ✓ Eye contact: Eyes are the windows to your feelings. Show concern
- ✓ Body posture: Informs the other person of your confidence as well as energy levels. The customer may not be impressed if you pose leaning against fixtures, desks or mannequins and maybe read this as a "don't care" attitude
- ✓ Grooming: How presentable and organized are you in the interaction?
- ✓ Facial expressions: Pleasant, warm and natural.
- ✓ Movement and Space: Visitors need to be given time and space without a feeling that you are breathing over them. It is important not to invade the customer's space.

Greeting politely is one thing, but rushing up close to the customer is quite another.

The professional should be sensitive to the customers' position by varying one's position and distance and observing whether this has any effect on them.

So let's begin with that first step of 'Greeting the customer'

This part has been included particularly for the larger outlets that also have a major retail showroom that displays all related products used and recommended. So, if you are a customer, I just want you to picture yourself walking into any store. How do you think the sales people would greet you (if at all)? One of the most common ways is: *'Good morning'* followed with a '*Can I help you?*' question. And what is your usual response to such a greeting

If you are familiar with the retail sector, you will know by now that one of the most common statements that will come from customers right up front when approached like this is: *'Oh, I'm just looking around'* and this puts the sales person off. It is a very common statement you'll hear in most show rooms and retail outlets. It is actually not an objection at all as most sales people think; but just a common defense mechanism or conditioned response that flows out. The truth is most customers are not interested in feeling pressurized into buying something. It's their way of moving away from the sales pressure that they are anticipating. Everyone has had a bad sales experience or two, and they want to avoid another if possible. Regardless of what they say, there is some level of intent and interest to make a purchase, and as an expert you need to maximize on this to help customers find the right product or service.

But before we get into handling this, we must get to understand where or why does this come from a majority of customers. Traditionally, we have seen people use this statement because they are scared of high pressure sales tactics and have probably had a bad experience with sales people who have pestered them in the past. They are afraid that if they tell the sales person up front of what they're looking for, that they will not have their freedom to browse at their own pace, without the sales person trying to impose on them into making a buying decision. They want to be able to have that freedom to just explore all options on their own.

Sometimes this statement could be genuine- the customer may actually just be looking; but most times, this statement is because they don't want to be pushed or influenced.

But trying to understand what the customer actually means when they say something like this: their purchase intent, and what stage are they in the purchase/ decision process is important. Understanding the customer's position will place you, the expert in a better position to help them find what they are looking for.

So here is what *"Oh, I'm just looking around…"* could at most times mean:

- ✓ *The customer is actually just looking*
- ✓ *The customer may already have a particular product in mind*
- ✓ *Maybe the customer is yet not sure how much the product will cost or how much they want to spend for it*
- ✓ *She has not decided as yet when she wants to make a purchase/ have a treatment*
- ✓ *Maybe the customer is not sure if he/she will make a purchase/ have a treatment at all*

All this could mean that a customer could be at various stages in the sales cycle, with some of them having no clue, while yet some know exactly what they want. You will begin to find eventually that there are three types of customers that walk into your store:

- ✓ *The Decided Customer*
- ✓ *The Undecided Customer*
- ✓ *The Browsing Customer*

The acronym C.A.R.E. standing for 'Customers are Really Everything' should tell us that by demonstrating that you genuinely care about the customer's situation can be crucial in serving and handling their needs- and this comes a lot from building rapport right up front by empathizing with them

Below is a simple process to handle the '*Oh, I'm just looking around*' sales objection.

The first step to handle this *"Oh, I'm just looking around*" is to make the customer feel warm and comfortable by welcoming them the right way (as we will cover very soon)- giving them the feeling of being able to look around, and then asking what you may be able to help them with. A word of caution though; not too very enthusiastically as this might just turn them off. Your greeting (which we will be seeing later) should be sincere, conveying that you are keen on helping them- not just to make a quick sale. Your body language, your tone and your choice of words should convey this

It is at this stage that you may get this statement coming from them:*"Oh, I'm just looking around"* And it is here where most salespeople make a big blunder of saying *'no problem'* and continue to move away, leaving the customer to do just that.

Instead the sales person would need to let the customer know that it is absolutely ok as most customers initially come into the store for just that. This way, you are now putting the customer at ease giving him/ her, the assurance that you are not going to push them into anything, but you are someone who is there to serve their needs.

While this positions you in the mind of the customer as someone who genuinely cares for them, it is also in the process moving in the direction of building rapport. You may like to simply follow up by asking the customer what they are looking for in particular; based on where the movements of their eyes are-you could refer to something unique about that particular product. By doing so, you have now strategically made them visualize what it is that they are looking for...

And once they begin to show interest, simply move into your next step of the G.R.E.A.T sales model, so that you can help learn why they want that product or solution in a consultative way.
You could use the 4 A's to also help you handle customers that come up with:*"Oh, I'm just looking around"*

- ✓ Assume
- ✓ Agree
- ✓ Assist
- ✓ Ask

1. Assume that they want to look around
Assume the customer wants to look around, and encourage them to do so with the various options that your outlet has- making them feel at ease and comfortable, with the assurance that you are there to help if there is anything specific they want to know more about.
2. Agree with Them
When a customer tells you he/she is just looking around, the most effective way is to agree with them, that you are happy that they have come in and decided to do it with your store. Demonstrate that you appreciate them taking the time to do so and thank them for picking your store
3. Assist them
Avoid the mistake of plunging into your sales pitch, as that will most certainly put them off. Keep reassuring them that you are available to assist them. If they show an interest, you could then request if you could ask them a few questions to understand their specific needs so that you would be in a better position to help them.
4. Ask them open questions

There are two types of questions as you will see in a later chapter, but for now, it is important to ask the right questions. Most sales personnel ask closed ended questions such as: *"Is there anything that I could help you with"* and this is why they end up with hearing that statement from the customer *"Oh, no thank you, I'm just looking around"*

Instead, by asking open-ended questions such as, *"Good day, what brings you in today?"* prevents that usual statement and opens the door for more. The key is to ask such questions genuinely and politely, otherwise it may just seem impolite and back fire. By observing the customer's body language, you will be in a position to assess how receptive they are about moving further..

So how should your greeting be?

Remember that you have only <u>one</u> opportunity to make a great first impression. 90% of lasting impressions are created in the first 90 seconds. The <u>first impression begins before</u> you even open your mouth to speak a single word to the customer. And as we've seen in an earlier chapter, you can't afford to miss this.

As the customer enters the store, he/she does a quick visual scan. They spot the sales person and their first mental picture is recorded...People go by what they see more than what they hear. That means that whatever the person is doing at that precise moment will influence their first impression (eg: Like the automobile training I mentioned of in an earlier chapter)

When customers walk into your store, they believe that they are giving you an opportunity to serve them and I believe the only way to align with the customer's thinking is to begin by 'thanking' the customer for coming to your facility. You're not just saying a general hello to them; but you're acknowledging them, appreciating them, grateful for their presence and conveying that you are excited to see them.

"Thanks for coming in" could honestly make anyone feel welcome. So if you want to change your customers' conditioned response (From *"Oh, I'm just looking around*"), then you would need to change your conditioned greeting to them (move away from *"How are you?"* or *"How can I help you?"* It's a conditioned greeting just as *"Just looking"* is a conditioned response.

You might like to mention your store name too: "*Good Evening, and welcome to Diadem Beauty Salon-The Haven for Gorgeous Looks!"* or *"Thank you for coming into Diadem Beauty Salon-The Haven for Gorgeous Looks!"*

"It's a great day at (Mention your Salon/ Spa), how can I make you happier today?

"Thank you for choosing (Your Spa name). With all the choices you have, we truly appreciate you choosing us."

You could get still more creative by having the guests names posted on your *'Welcome Board".* Imagine how your customers would feel as they arrive to see their names displayed on your welcome board.

You could further surprise your guests, as they are take on a tour around the salon/ spa, by inviting them to enter their names or drop their business cards into a draw for a free service/ treatment, which could be once a month

Avoid the pitfall of using the same greeting repeatedly. Use a variety of greetings during the day. You could comment on their clothing or ask about the parking, but be enthusiastic and sincere. Everyone loves to be complimented, acknowledged and appreciated, so why not start off the customer's experience with you on a high note by making them feel great, being welcomed and valued?

Greeting your customer by name and using her name throughout your time of interaction together is a great feeling. Everyone loves to hear their own name. What could be more personal? You are demonstrating interest in the customer, by indicating that you know her and care for her.

Research shows that 80% of customers long to be welcomed with a friendly greeting.

Here some other ways to greet your customers

- ✓ *"Welcome back! How have you been?"* This greeting works well for customers you are familiar with or know very well. You can go on to ask how he or she liked the product they purchased and if they are buying another. This also shows that you recognize them. If you know their names, better still. *"Mrs. Jackson, you're back! We are so happy to have you with us again! Welcome!"*
- ✓ Offer a sincere compliment: This could be one of the most difficult greetings, but when given sincerely, a compliment can really engage your customer. Make it relevant or specific to your business, such as *"That's a very pretty shade of nail polish you are using"* This must be done genuinely, for if not, it could be construed as being phony and you may lose the most important thing you need to sell-trust.
- ✓ Use a conversation starter item: An interesting product on display, painting, carving or

sculpture, or anything you have near your entrance that draws comment is a great way to start. Some examples being:

"Are you aware that we have the largest selection of... in this area?"

"We offer that in a variety of packs/ treatments"

"That Therapy has some very useful benefits you might be interested in"

It gets the customer talking, questioning and Interested.

Most importantly, a customer service greeting should flow like a normal conversation. If you are greeting a customer face to face, remember to always follow social guidelines such as respecting personal space and volume of voice. This may vary from country to country- so be aware of such etiquette and cultures too.

Dealing with an Incoming Call/ Greeting Customers

Here are some ways that you could greet customers that call your salon/ spa. Learn to build variety depending on the seasons, times and offers in place. Keep a data bank of such greetings!

- ✓ *"It's a great day at* (Mention your Salon/ Spa), *how can I make you happier today?*
- ✓ *"Thank you for choosing (*Your Spa name). *With all the choices you have, we truly appreciate you choosing us."*
- ✓ *"Thank you for choosing* (Your salon name), *this is Sarah. How may I assist you today?"*

The person answering the phone can get very creative too*:* If it's a salon, then here is a creative way of greeting!

- ✓ *"Love is in the hair at Sparkling Colors Salon, this is Sarah, how may I assist you?"*

One of the more professional ways to deal with customers on line is to avoid giving out too much information over the telephone. The best way is to gain contact information and invite the client to your location, where you have a better chance of closing them on using your various salon/ spa services.

Here is a typical flow of what could take place:

Receptionist: *It's wonderful out here at* (your salon name), *this is (*first name only of receptionist) *how may I help you?*

Customer: *I am calling regarding* (customer mentions a treatment/ therapy).

Receptionist: *Perfect, that's one of our very popular treatments. Are you already familiar with the treatment process?*

Depending on the customer response of yes or no…you proceed with the next step Avoid discussing price or giving too much information over the phone.

If answer is a 'NO', the Receptionist may respond with: '*To better help you understand the process, I would like to invite you in for a free consultation with our one of our specialists to enable us better understand your specific needs and what would be most beneficial for you. We have openings this weekend and beginning of next week. Which would you prefer? The mornings or afternoons? I have an open slot at (time) and another at (time). Which one would you prefer?'*

If answer is a 'YES', the Receptionist may respond with: *That's great! When would you like to schedule an appointment- this week or next? Do you prefer mornings or afternoons? I notice that I have an open*

slot at (time) and another at (time) - which one would you prefer?
Customer: *(Picks a day and a time)*
Receptionist: '*Wonderful! Just to reconfirm- The time is… on… You said your first name is…..How do I spell your last name correctly please? And should we need to reach you, then xxxxxx is your cell phone to call you on? Is that right?'*
Customer: *Yes, perfect!*
Receptionist: '*Thank you very much. And I'm having a confirmation message sent to you right now along with a link to a map providing directions- just in case you may need the directions. Is there anything else that I could assist with?'*
Customer: '*No, nothing really…you've been extremely helpful'*
Receptionist: '*Thank you very much Ms.* (name of customer) *and look forward to seeing you on …* (date)'

It is best advisable that the receptionist does not get into any recommendations, but helps the client move into a consultation first with something like this when the prospective client asks about having a facial service: *"Ms Jackson, as you are aware, Sparkling Colors Salon, specializes in corrective skin therapy and in fact have many types of treatment, however to determine which treatment would be most beneficial for your skin health, we ideally begin with a consultation and analysis… this ensures that you receive the best expert therapy for your skin type and conditions"*
Assuming the answer is positive, the receptionist now continues: *"Ms Jackson I have booked you in with Amanda (aesthetician's name), she's an*

excellent aesthetician and all her clients rave about her treatments as she is so knowledgeable…she will also give you loads of helpful advice on how to keep your skin looking and feeling great. In fact she has recently awarded the Excellence Award at the Beauticians Association. And while you are here can I schedule you in for a lash and brow tint with this appointment and will you also be having a brow wax?"

(**Note what this Smart Receptionist has done:** Through her friendly professional attitude she has demonstrated enthusiasm for the salon, its treatments and co-workers by doing the "ground-work" and building up for her co-workers abilities and has even up-sold from a facial to include extra services)

Remember: Your Words make a Difference!

Asking questions such as, *"What kind of service can I schedule for you?"* versus *"What do you want to get done?"* makes a difference between three star and five star services. Phrases like "absolutely" and "our pleasure" should replace common phrases like "sure" and "yes." This type of positive, enthusiastic language must be the norm at your salon/ spa

Here are some more examples to watch for:

"Oh, we're out of stock."	"We're completely sold out".
"We can't get any until next month."	"They're selling so fast we can't keep them in stock!"
"All we have left is this piece".	"We have a display unit available right now".
"You can try getting it at one of our other showrooms."	"Let me contact one of our other stores and see if they can help".
"We can order that, but it will take three to four weeks for delivery."	"We can order that for you and have it in just three to four weeks".

Use Positive Speech to Demonstrate Empathy

- ✓ I don't know (Instead say, '*That's a good question, Let me find out for you*', or offer to get back, after finding the answer...')
- ✓ 'I/we can't do that. (Instead use positive statements, such as, '*This is what I/we can do.')*
- ✓ 'You will have to' (Instead say, '*you'll need to*, or '*I need you to'* or '*Here's how we can help you'*)
- ✓ Instead of 'Sorry to keep you waiting' (which evokes a mental response of '*You* should be'), say, *'Thank you for waiting/holding.*

Never keep customers waiting

If you recall in one of the earlier chapters, I covered an example of me visiting an automobile showroom, without announcing my trip (as a ghost customer), and the time it took before the team acknowledged my presence. Well, a business study carried out recently, recorded the amount of time people had to wait to be greeted in several business locations- and when asked how long they had been waiting before someone came to acknowledge their presence- the customers' estimates of time elapsed were much longer than actual time. A customer waiting 30 or 40 seconds often feels like it's been three or four minutes. Time drags when you are waiting, especially when you know you are the one going to be paying for a service.

No matter how busy you are with another customer or on a phone, pause for a moment just to say hello, making eye contact and making sure you have the loveliest smile on your face no matter how bad your day could have been. Let the customer know that you will be with them soon, with a simple *"I'll be with you in a minute,"* and a smile. If you can't greet them right away, your smile should compensate and buy you a few seconds. This can go a long way and save a customer from having less than that super experience that she came in for.

Putting the client at ease

When a client visits the salon, it is very important that they are: Comfortable with their surroundings, at ease with their therapist/ beautician and that you treat them with consideration, respect and courtesy. Listen attentively and actively to what they have to say. These factors are key to building a regular clientele. The client must receive a high level of customer service from the moment they enter the door until the moment they leave.

Here are some essential points to remember for every service:

- ✓ Make appropriate eye contact, but do not stare at them so intently that they begin to feel uncomfortable.
- ✓ Use body language that is open and welcoming – e.g. smiling, leaning forward to show your interest – but do not overdo it as it may feel threatening. Read the client's body language, e.g. facial expressions and gestures.
- ✓ Sit if they are sitting-it can feel very intimidating to have someone standing over you and talking to you; it can feel as though they are talking at you.
- ✓ Sit where you can be seen without the client having to turn to see you– arrange chairs so

that you are at a slight angle, where each of you can comfortably see the other one.

- ✓ Treat the client appropriately during interruptions (e.g. from colleagues or other clients).

EXERCISE: ***From the examples in this chapter, work on developing your own set of Greetings…Have at least 5 to 6 different varieties that you could use, depending on the customer and situation***

R- Revealing Questions
The Consultation Process Begins
(Understanding their Needs)

The second and a very important step of the G.R.E.A.T. Sales Model is to ask 'Revealing Questions', which is to uncover the customer's specific needs. This step and the next can really make that big difference between you and the competition.

Before we get into trying to uncover the customer's need, we must first have an understanding of how customers buy- the psychology behind every purchase.

Human needs are segmented based on their priority and only once the lower level human needs are met, human beings move up to the next level. Human beings are motivated to fulfill their needs in a hierarchy. It begins with the most basic needs before moving on to advanced needs.

Here is a typical thought pattern when it comes to any major purchase:

- ✓ Need Recognition-Any purchase of product/ service begins with recognizing a need. People have various needs: birthday, wedding, party, relaxation, de-stress, or just a makeover are only a few examples
- ✓ Information is sought: Search begins through net, friends, relatives, recommendations etc
- ✓ Interest is personalized: Options are explored-making key decisions about their requirements and their preferences

- ✓ Interest at its peak: Various alternatives are evaluated from the several options that suit their interests and now ready to choose the ideal one.
- ✓ Interest modified by price if needed
- ✓ That's it- I will purchase it/ I am getting this done! The person decides to go forward with the purchase/ treatment. This is when they call to schedule an appointment
- ✓ Post Purchase: This is a key stage as it is the perfect time to request for referrals and testimonials.

A smart professional must understand these stages and work accordingly

- ✓ To arouse interest
- ✓ To impart knowledge (of service or properties)
- ✓ To personalize (customer benefits)
- ✓ To stimulate the desire (to possess)
- ✓ To satisfy (price worth and objections)
- ✓ To work on advocacy

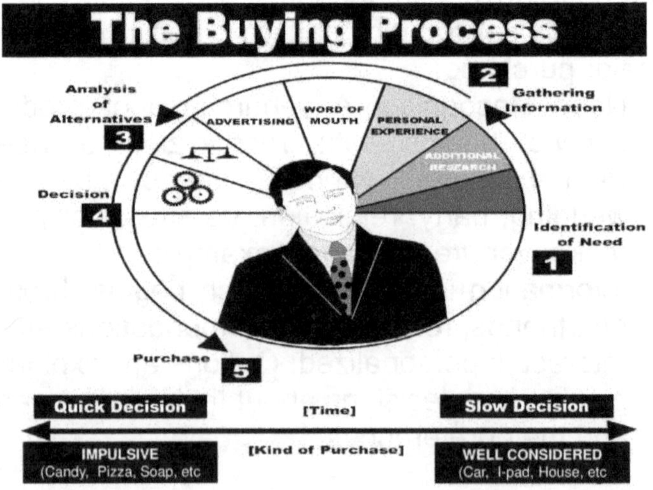

The illustration clearly depicts the process in the mind of a buyer when making a decision to purchase anything and as can be seen for smaller items (such as a cake of soap- one does not have to think or ponder about this purchase) as the decisions are usually quick and impulsive, whereas for costlier, well considered ones (such as purchasing a car) the process obviously may take some more time.

Every customer that enters a facility comes in to fulfill two specific needs: **Logical and Emotional**

Neuroscientists have determined that emotions such as love, feelings, vanity, looks and pride can play a central role in this entire process. The way we feel can help determine what decisions we make and why. Part of the role of a therapist/ beautician is to help the client navigate through the big emotions that come along with deciding.

While emotions will always play a part, rational or logical decisions must also factor in. When making logical or rational decisions, we often consider things like discounts, profit, security/ safety, ease of use and health. Emotional ones relate to the customer's ego and feelings of satisfaction, looks, sentiments, relief, success, pride and joy.

These are the needs that mostly push or motivate the customer to buy and are the key to moving forward in a sale

Remember: *People buy EMOTIONALLY, but justify with LOGIC*

Here are some specific examples for Emotional Reasons

- ✓ Fear: *Of competition, of being left behind, of others doing better, fear of ill-health/not being fit*

- ✓ Love: *Desiring the approval of colleagues, family and friends*
- ✓ Entertainment: *Enjoyment, relaxation etc.*
- ✓ Sentimental: *Family tradition, something close to your heart.*
- ✓ Pride: *Being associated with a successful name/ brand/ style/pattern*
- ✓ Pleasure: *Derived from the appearance of the new purchase/ treatment, etc*
- ✓ Envy: *Of others' successful achievements*
- ✓ Vanity: *Recognition by others of having made a wise decision*

While many personnel are champs at trying to uncover *what* customers want in services/ products (which is the logical need), they fail however to find out *why* the customer is utilizing or making that particular purchase of service or product. They don't learn or try to understand what is the inner driving force that will make the customer to buy; which are the emotional needs- and to determine a customer's emotional need requires the person to get answers to questions like:

- ✓ *Why has she chosen this outlet in particular?*
- ✓ *What specifically is the customer looking for?*
- ✓ *What will make her feel good?*
- ✓ *What is her preferred choice, any specific reason as to why?*

Most people avoid uncovering this powerful psychological area- either out of sheer ignorance or they feel it could be a waste of time and may irritate customers; but it is very important to try and understand how a customer will feel after a purchase has been made. Successful professionals can actually have customers visualize scenes of after the purchase and how the customer will be using the product- enabling actual ownership before really buying it.

And by getting to understand the customer's need accurately and thoroughly, you will help build an instant bonding, trust and relationship that can lead and last to help the customer come back and keep referring you to others. But this is one step that the majority of people try to avoid as it does take time, energy, dedication and discipline. But as a professional, this is what will give you that edge over others.

So it is important to tune into the client's concerns. *Why did they come, what would they like to change about their appearance or lifestyle, what services are they interested in, what expectations do they have, and are those expectations realistic?*

The answers to these questions should give you some indication of the client's lifestyle, overall health, products they use, skin care regime, and personality. Don't be afraid to ask them what they like and don't like and what is working and what is not. When you are truly present and clients feel they have been heard, they feel special and cared for—and will always come back- knowing that you care for them!

To be able to do this effectively, you will need to get into a Professional Consulting Process

The Consulting Process

When you begin consulting, there are a few key areas to note, and having the acronym **S.O.A.P** in mind can help you stay on track. However, before you even begin the process, you must keep in mind that this examination process can be very scary for some clients and therefore you might like to put the customer at ease with a compliment about the client's skin, hair or one of their features; before you start the process

S stands for **Subjective** information. Areas/ Issues that the client feels, complains about, problems they present, and so on. For example, has their skin felt itchy, burning or have they felt dry or dehydrated lately?

O stands for **Objective**, which are things you actually see or the observable findings. For example -what do you notice about the skin- dry, dehydrated and flaking skin with fine lines? Observation comes with a lot of practice

A stands for **Assessment**. What treatments are you recommending to address the above identified concerns?

P stands for **Plan**. What are the short- and long-term plans you need to develop to resolve these issues and any chances of these spreading elsewhere? Will they return for future treatments? What will be the at-home treatments/what type of follow-up are you planning to recommend?

Before we get any further, there's one key point to adhere to when consulting and that is: *Always show confidentiality during discussion by not breaking that of others.*

How great sales opportunities are missed by not following the above?

Here is a typical example of how sales opportunities are lost: Let's say, the customer has booked for a facial and although the therapist handling the customer observes that the skin would benefit from a more advanced treatment she does not recommend her client for upgraded treatment. The customer walks out only with the treatment booked for- very much under-serviced. In this instance the therapist could have created a sales opportunity and delivered a much superior treatment to the client, thus, opening up on further opportunities through retailing of products too and a service that the customer will be thankful for later as she sees the results.

To prevent misconceptions and misunderstandings, it is crucial to pay special attention to new clients- so you won't have to redo the service and it will not only save you time and money, but it will also establish a foundation for future business by fostering confidence in her.

Opening up on Possibilities

Immense opportunities can open up with simple statements like, *"Ms. Jones, while you are here for your brow wax can I offer you a complimentary skin analysis, it will only take a few minutes and it's important to check your skins' health condition at the change of every season".* This simple yet powerful statement opens up on the possibility for treatment and retail sales. The more consultations and analysis the higher the service and retail sales will be and is the therapist's key information gathering technique. It reveals areas of treatment need and identifies gaps or non-existing areas in home care regimes.

Also, this could be a great time to recommend a program/ treatment or series of treatments (to ensure maximum results) for regular maintenance.

Remember that the best form of advertising for you and the salon is a client who leaves the establishment delighted with her experience. This client will undoubtedly recommend you to family and friends, which will bring in additional business. And for this to happen and guarantee that the consultation is successful, you must increase the client's trust and comprehension, by ensuring that there is never any opportunity for misunderstanding or conflict because you and your client must be on the same understanding-having the same goals for the outcome.

Asking Questions and Listening

To ensure that the factors mentioned above are uncovered effectively, there are two key components that are vital: **Asking questions and listening attentively are the Keys**

A very important step is to ask 'Revealing Questions', which is to uncover the customer's specific needs, wants, expectations, dreams or pains/ issues that the customer has. The purpose of this step is to obtain information that will allow you to move to the next step in the sales process. It is based on the principle that *"People will tell you anything you want to know-all you have to do is ask"*

Why do we ask questions?

- ✓ To gain control
- ✓ To uncover the customer's needs
- ✓ To understand the customer more and help build rapport
- ✓ To isolate areas of interest
- ✓ To get minor agreements
- ✓ To arouse emotions
- ✓ To isolate objections
- ✓ To answer objections
- ✓ To demonstrate that you really care and not just pushing your thoughts

By getting to understand the customer's need accurately and thoroughly, you can anticipate fewer or no objections later in the process. This is one step that the majority of people try to avoid as it does take time, energy, dedication professionalism and discipline. But as a professional, this is what will give you that edge over others.

Effective Questioning

When trying to unravel needs, it must be done in a logical pattern that will bring the customer to a stage of realization that there is a problem or need.

So the art of uncovering needs requires the use of different types of questions. So let us have an understanding of the different types of questions that we could ask someone. Though there are several types of questions, for the purpose of this exercise let us look at just the two most important ones ie;

OPEN-ended Questions

CLOSED-ended Questions

Depending on what type of answer you want from the other person, either of these questions are used.

Eg; If I asked you: *'Did you have your dinner'?*

Or *'Do you like this training session?'* or *'Are you going home this evening'?*

The only possible answer that you could give me would either be a *'yes'* or a *'no'*

That is why this type of a question is called a 'closed question', because the only possible answer would be a one word- with either a *'yes'* or *'no'*

Closed questions usually begin with:

'Are you…'

'Will you…'

'Do you…'

'Would you…'

Most people ask the wrong questions-Closed questions-that only get a 'yes' or 'no' as a response:

- ✓ "Do you want this?"
- ✓ "Is this something you'd be interested in?"
- ✓ "Our new Packs/ specialized Treatments have… would you like that?"

Closed questions go straight to the point and don't provide an opportunity for customers to express themselves. For example, *'So, if I trim about an inch off the sides, would that be what you'd like?'*
In this case the only possible answer would be *"yes that's fine"* They are usually not very helpful in starting a conversation and extracting information. They can however be useful at a certain time, which you will see later in this chapter. But most sales people are more comfortable asking such questions, which we need to avoid at this stage.
The opposite of 'closed' is the obvious: 'open'.
Open-ended questions allow the customer to open up or do the talking and are used to encourage a client to speak freely about a concern or expand on something already raised during the conversation
Always remember this: Open Questions generally begin with 5W's and 1 H ie;
Who?
What?
When?
Where?
Why?
How?
And they encourage the other person to open up and speak.
If we were to redo that example again using open questions, they would go something like this: *'What did you have for dinner?' 'How do you feel about this training?' 'What plans do you have for this evening'?*
These questions will certainly not fetch you a *'yes'* or *'no'* like how closed questions do. But they would allow the other person to open up with information which is what you as a sales person requires.

For example, if you are considering color, you might ask, *'When you say you don't like too much of a bright color, what exactly do you mean, could you explain that a bit more?'* You could further help the client by showing her color charts that you need to have ready by your side.

Here are some more examples of effective qualifying questions

- ✓ What are you looking for in a ...?
- ✓ What particularly interests you?
- ✓ Why are those important to you?
- ✓ What brings you into our salon or spa today?
- ✓ What was your experience at...?
- ✓ What do/did you like or dislike about your previous experience?
- ✓ How do you plan to use your....?

Dealing with various customer situations:

Because most personnel do not ask the right questions up front, and after spending a lot of time with the customer, they get frustrated or angry when a customer would tell them that she would need to check with her husband, or have the job redone or the sales person finds out that the customer is not planning to move forward with the treatment!

Learn to wear the RIGHT Hat!

From customer to customer and even within the same customer presentation, GREAT Retail Sales and Service Personnel instinctively know which role to take on:

The Type of Call	The Role
✓ "I'd like to know/have... Please send me..."	**Provider**
✓ "What should I do about...? How can I...?" Which would you?"	**Advisor**

- ✓ Distressed customer needing empathy, understanding and reassurance — **Supporter**
- ✓ Getting the customer out of a challenging situation — **Rescuer**
- ✓ Solving the customer's problem and complaint — **Problem Solver**

To switch between and perform each of these roles you need to ask questions and listen actively.

Here is a list of some more examples of open-ended questions:

- ✓ What results do you expect from… or What are your objectives for…
- ✓ What are your expectations from your treatment today?
- ✓ What are your real skin care concerns?
- ✓ What skin care products are you currently using?
- ✓ What is your level of sun exposure?
- ✓ How long is it until the wedding/party/holiday?
- ✓ How do you want to look on your big day?
- ✓ What are your worries about your party? How can we help you?

Some Examples of Closed Questions

As we've seen, closed probes are used to obtain an agreement, a commitment, or a tightly controlled response. For example,

- ✓ Would you agree that…?
- ✓ Would you like to improve…?

- ✓ Are you taking any medications? Do you have any medical conditions, including but not limited to: skin
- ✓ Do you have any allergies?
- ✓ Have you seen any pictures of how you would like to look, as a guide for make-up, eyebrow shape and nails?
- ✓ Is this for a special occasion? Do you have a particular style in mind?

Shooting out open questions without any logical order would also be inappropriate, as it could be unprofessional, could be irritating at times and most of all cause confusion in the mind of the customer. But if the customer was taken through a logical pattern, it could help lead her or open up to an understanding of her own situation, problem or need- that many times she may not be aware of.

The logical pattern has 3 parts:

Current Situation

Desired Situation

Barriers

The current situation is usually where the customer is at or what they are currently using and starts with questions like: '*What has she been using? Are they currently using one? For how long and how satisfied is she*'?

This is where they are **'now'** and so we usually recommend that you do not ask many of these.

We then gradually move to the **'Desired Situation'** of where does the customer want to be or should be, with questions like *'What would they like the ideal product/ service levels to be or have'* or *'What would they like to see or have from....'* The answers to these questions will tell us the customer's future plans/ desires or where they should be or want to be. The next set of questions, are pertaining to the '**Barriers'** that are in his way, that are preventing her from reaching the desired situation and making the purchase now. This is the key that will enable her open her eyes. Sometimes, just one question here could open up opportunities. Barrier questions most times begin with: *'So what is preventing you from... "What is stopping you from...What is coming in the way to..."*

EXERCISE: ***Now keeping your customer in mind, look at building at least 5 open-ended questions each for 'Current' and 'Desired' and maybe 3 for 'Barriers***

-Current

-Desired

-Barriers

What should the sequential pattern be at this stage?

1. A good way to begin is always start with open questions
   (Using the questioning patterns mentioned above ie; Current, Desired, Barriers)
2. Listen attentively
3. Take notes if possible
4. Clarify/ reconfirm with closed questions

A professional expert ideally follows a sequential pattern at this stage, starting with Open Questions to uncover the specific needs, particularly focusing on the emotional side. While the customer talks, you as a professional would need to listen attentively.

'People were designed with two ears and one mouth, and that is the ratio in which to use them'!

How to be a good listener?

One of the greatest skills that you as an expert can develop is the skill of listening. The best experts are the ones that do less talking and more of listening and that is why I believe God gave us two ears and one mouth- so we would do more listening than talking!

Here are some keys to be an "active" listener:

- ✓ Suspend judgment, initially- Keep an open mind
- ✓ Focus on the speaker and what he/she is saying
- ✓ Never interrupt while the customer speaks
- ✓ Tolerate silence. Silence can initially be uneasy, but if you practice tolerating it, you will find it very beneficial especially when negotiating.
- ✓ Listen for facts and key words
- ✓ Observe their body posture, facial expressions and gestures
- ✓ Avoid distractions and never carry on side conversations
- ✓ Give your undivided attention, listening not only to the words, but how they are spoken – the tone of voice, the pace and emphasis and the 'feelings behind the words'
- ✓ Show that you are actively listening by your facial expression, gestures, eye contact and 'verbal encouragers', such as *'Mmm' or 'What happened then?'*,
- ✓ Assess what you've heard
- ✓ Take notes of key points

- ✓ Clarify and reconfirm what the customer has told you- never assume!
- ✓ Never attempt doing anything else while with a customer! The phone is a big disturbance and bad manners

Before you respond, assess the information you heard by asking yourself four questions in your mind:

- ✓ *What has the customer told me?*
- ✓ *What can I do with this information?*
- ✓ *What else do I need to know?*
- ✓ *What questions do I still need to ask?*

To show you're listening actively:

- ✓ Respond by using terms like, *'Go on'*, *Uh huh'* and '*mmm*'
- ✓ Stay always tuned and alert

To show that you have, understood:

- ✓ Use, phrases like *"I see," "I understand"*
- ✓ Paraphrase, *"So you want me to …"*

EXERCISE: *What are the areas that you would need to work on to improve your listening skills beginning from your very next appointment? List out and make a dedicated effort to work on these.*

Taking Notes

A professional expert will always take notes of key points and never depend on memory. You may upfront itself indicate to the customer that you are taking notes: *"Is it okay Ms. Customer, if I jot down a few notes as we go along"*

By asking to take notes and doing so, you are subtly indicating to the customer:

- ✓ *I care about you and your well being*
- ✓ *I do not want to miss anything*

- ✓ *The customer may have visited/ or may visit the competition, and she will now see the difference, as they were more interested in the business- but you are indicating: 'I am here to help' 'I am a professional'*

Clarifying and Reconfirming with Closed Questions

After asking the right questions, listening, and fully understanding what the customer is looking for we should now verbally summarize. This is the time when closed questions are very useful. To clarify and reconfirm, restate in your own words what the client has said and ask him to verify your understanding.

- ✓ *"From what you have told me, here's what you are looking… You want a….is that right?"*
- ✓ *"So based on what you have said, these are the most important…... You would like… Would that be accurate?"*
- ✓ *"So, if I trim about an inch off the sides, would that be what you'd like?'*

Clarifying and reconfirming with these type of closed questions can help you pin-point exactly the requirement or understanding…for example: How short is short? How red is red? What does the client exactly mean?

Only after the customer has confirmed your understanding, you have earned the right to proceed with additional questions to gain more information about the situation.

These types of closed questions can help you even as you are completing your service, by helping you to always clarify the client's expectations, such as *"I will give you more texture on the crown to help create*

more body and lift" or *"I will darken your eyebrows to help give a better frame for your eyes."*
As a beautician, it is your responsibility to always make sure the client is happy with the final outcome. For example, if they feel their hair is too long, you should cut it a little shorter until they are fully satisfied; if they feel their lipstick is too dark, you should either blot it and apply a lighter shade on top or remove it and apply a new shade.

Why summarize regularly?

- ✓ *It keeps complexities under control*
- ✓ *It tests progress*
- ✓ *It lets you restate what the other party has said*
- ✓ *It can help gain the initiative*
- ✓ *It can keep the discussion on track*
- ✓ *It can prevent misinterpretation, misunderstanding and subsequent bitterness*
- ✓ *In other words, summarizing helps you stay on top (but you take the point).*

By summarizing, you are making sure you have the right information and that you haven't left out anything.

Finally…One simple technique: *Focus!*
If you focus on your customers, the ones that ultimately pay your salaries, then you will….

-Hear what they say,
-Will understand what they are looking for,
-Will build rapport with them,
-And will set yourself apart from the competition

E- Explain, Enlighten, Engage, Enthuse and Excite Customers about your Service/ Product

"People don't care how much you know until they know how much you care"

The third step in the GREAT Sales Model and another very important step is to 'Explain your Product/ Service and Prove its Value' in the mind of the customer.

Usually the temptation for a person at this stage, once she has identified the need is to immediately jump into recommending the solution. This can backfire with a number of objections, as the customer is yet not convinced on the value of your proposition. Therefore, there is one more step, before we actually get to recommend your solution; to build in the mind of the customer the value that your company and the product or service that matches the relevant need identified brings to them.

It is similar to what a good waiter would do in a restaurant. Before he takes your order he would literally make your mouth water by talking about the taste of the dishes by building up that appetite in you. So now when he does bring the dish to the table, you are ready to relish it!

Explaining your Product and Proving its value is the process of showing your customer how specific features of your product or service can offer benefits that will help your customer meet their need, solve a problem or realize an opportunity that you had identified in the earlier step. The purpose is to demonstrate to the customer the value of your product or service. Not all customers will be sure of the value; particularly new customers. Therefore by proving value, it allows you to show the customer why your product or service is an effective one and the value it brings to them, before you show the customer how you can help them solve a problem/need or realize an opportunity with your recommendation.

Whenever people buy anything, there are two aspects that they are concerned about:

1. *What will the relevant product or service do for me- how will it help me? What value will we get from this?*
2. *Who or Which is the company behind this? Their standing? Will they support me when I need them? The Reliability factor!*

Let us look at the Product or Service first:

There are 3 aspects to any product or service. The **Features, Advantages** and **Benefits**

A Feature describes some '*characteristics*' of a product or service. Features are relatively neutral, both in their content and in their effect on the buyer. Features are those aspects of a product, or service that we can see, or describe. It is usually what the manufacturer or producer '*has put into*' the product.

Let us take 2 Examples:

The first one as a common example (not related to the beauty trade- to help even a novice build this understanding) and the second one pertaining to this sector

- ✓ *This mobile phone has a 'hands-free' facility*
- ✓ *This pack contains green tea extract.*

When presenting features, it is important to emphasize only those features that are most important to the customer and for the treatment being provided. It must relate to the customers' buying criteria.

Now a number of personnel lose out big time because they just rattle 'only' the features of the product or service they are representing. It is not enough for the professional to rattle off the list of peptides, vitamins, botanicals, and other actives in the tube or jar. . And because of this the customer does not see the perceived value, because sometimes this could just sound technical and go over her head!

They must on the other hand in addition, have an accurate, detailed knowledge of *why* these ingredients are important, how they work, and how they benefit the skin or the customer. This is especially important with regard to skin care product ingredients. We therefore need to translate each relevant feature into an ultimate 'Benefit' where the customer will be able to see value. In other words '*what will it do'* for the customer!

Again, some people make the mistake of mentioning all of the features of the product or service that they could think of during their presentation. This is not helpful at all, but on the contrary confusing and can actually deter the customer from making a positive buying decision. It can indicate that the person wasn't listening effectively during the questioning phase of the sales process.

So as a professional expert, it is for you now to translate this relevant Feature or Features that you just spoke of into an Advantage. An Advantage describes how a product, or a product feature, can be used or can help the buyer during the buying process.

Advantages, as you will see are more persuasive than features. ***Salespeople who talk about advantages sell more than salespeople who just feature dump.***

Building on the same examples:

- ✓ *Because this mobile has a hand-free facility, you can use it safely to answer calls, while driving when the car is on the move*
- ✓ *This pack contains green tea extract, which is a powerful antioxidant.*

At this stage, we need to remind ourselves that people buy because they have needs.

If you as the seller can relate the product or service specifically to those needs identified in the earlier step, then there is a high probability of making a sale.

Benefits describe how the features and advantages will affect the buyer individually. They relate to the emotional buying behavior. In other words, the key is: ***what will the product or service do*** for them!

The key benefit words and statements are reassurance, confidence and peace of mind.

Asking questions in the earlier stage was to identify needs. Once we have identified the buyers' main buying criteria we can link the appropriate Features to the relevant Advantages and Benefits.

Think **FAB!**

Going back now to our earlier examples…

- ✓ *Because our mobile has a hand-free facility you can be confident that if a customer calls you in the car, you can respond to the call quickly and safely and not miss out on vital enquiries or business opportunities, thus not losing out on your business.*
- ✓ *This pack contains green tea extract, which is a powerful antioxidant and these antioxidants*

are helpful in offsetting and preventing the damage created by free radicals such as ultraviolet radiation, sunlight, cigarette smoke, and other environmental stressors that can age the skin.

Here is another example on all the benefits of a 'Massage Therapy'!

- ✓ *Relieves Stress*
- ✓ *Encourages Relaxation*
- ✓ *Improves Posture*
- ✓ *Improves Circulation*
- ✓ *Lower Blood Pressure*
- ✓ *Relaxes Muscles*
- ✓ *Improves Flexibility and Range of Motion*
- ✓ *Promotes Deeper and Easier Breathing*
- ✓ *Relieves Headaches*
- ✓ *Strengthens the Immune System*
- ✓ *Enhances Post-Operative Rehabilitation*
- ✓ *Improves Rehabilitation After Injury*

As you can see these are only the outlines of each benefit. You could even go further and mention how/ where each of these can help the client.

A good exercise to carry out at your spa/ salon/ health club is to list all your services and key products. Try outlining as many benefits you can come up with for each of these products. Keep this as a 'Prompt Sheet' in front you, to help you with every customer. Over a period of time, as you get thorough, you will not need this any longer.

EXERCISE: ***List all the relevant features of your product / service. Then translate each of the respective features into an Advantage and a***

Benefit. (Start with Skin/ Body Care Products such as: Cleansers, Toners, Moisturizers, Masks, Eye Care Serums, Corrective Treatments Exfoliants, Sun Protection, Body Care, Nail Care Products etc REMEMBER: The relevant benefit must address the Question: *"What's in it for the Customer?"* And must address 1 or more of the 5 P's seen above.

<u>Features</u> <u>Advantages</u> <u>Benefits</u>

Every business or individual has one or more of the 5 main needs and your Benefit must address <u>one</u> or <u>more</u> of these …they are the **5** P's…

Profit- to make/ save more money- through discounts/ offers, cost reductions, lesser medical costs, etc

Protection- to ensure the security and safety of their health, body, home, family, business, lives etc,

Peace-A good night's sleep with no botheration or worry

Prestige- Wanting to stand out- Image/ looks/ feel good factor!

Performance- Improved productivity, more efficiency, better stamina, less ageing etc

In the example that we covered earlier, you will notice that the customer benefits by:

1. Business calls that could come in while he is driving, leading to more revenue!
2. Safety while driving
3. To some- even prestigious using a 'hands-free' and driving (though I do not recommend it)

What is one phone call worth to him? If on an average he gets 10 business calls when driving, that could be the amount of business potential he could be missing out each day, if not attended to. So now the customer begins to see value in this feature of the product.

Exercise: Now in the second example on beauty about the product with the green tea extract; keeping the 5 P's in mind, can you as an exercise, point out the specific areas that the customer will find value and benefit from using it?

Ultimately, it is like an 'FM Radio Frequency' existing between the Buyer and Seller! **'WII-FM'** with the customer always sending out signals of... **W**hat **I**s **In** **I**t **F**or **M**e?

And until this Question is answered by the stylist/ beautician or therapist, the customer not be convinced and may never proceed!

What to keep in mind when working on solutions...

- ✓ The customer's vision/goals/ aspirations/ dreams-short term/ long term
- ✓ The customer's key challenges/ pains and requirements.
- ✓ Include advice and recommendations based on your client's own view of their hair, nails or skin type and condition.
- ✓ Use stylebooks, pictures, video clips as visual aids. People go by what they see more than what they hear. The retention is higher.

As mentioned, the other aspect of Proving Value has to do with the company that is backing the relevant product or service.

When Proving Value of your Company, it is important to keep in mind the USP's of your company or the respective manufacturer of that product that the customer wishes to buy–otherwise called as 'Unique Selling Propositions'...*What is it that makes your company/ or the manufacturer stand out from the others. What is so special about your company? Why should the customer move from his current vendor/ other stores to deal with your company?*

Your USP's have to be strong enough for it to draw the customer to you!

This is your key. What is it that makes your spa/ salon/ health club stand out? This takes some thinking...And as you identify your USP, remember that it can be just about anything that is unique and provides value to the customer: Examples could be a proprietary product created exclusively by you or one that is exclusive; an exclusive treatment method; or just that your spa is ecologically conscious, using only nature-based treatment products, earth-friendly décor and cleaning products; linens that are recyclable. Other general ones could include, the stability of your company/ expertise, years of standing, alliances and partnerships including awards and recognitions

There are many other ways to establish a unique selling position. Whatever be it, it has to ultimately work best for your spa by answering the needs of your clientele with an economically viable marketing plan that results in extraordinary consumer value.

EXERCISE: Try listing as many USP's that you can think of that differentiates your company/ store from the competition

Retailing Products

What do you think is the main reason why many therapists, stylists, beauticians/ estheticians hold back or are prevented from retailing to their customers? Studies show that there are two primary reasons that hold back these experts from retailing. The number one reason is “fear of rejection.” Human beings usually hate a ‘no’ for an answer, and this has come from past rejections that are now built-in as mental blocks. The second reason is “the perception of being too pushy.”

But if done the right way, at the right time, this can not only bring in enormous results in terms of enhancement of business, but help in customer satisfaction and retention, while building the overall confidence of the expert

Every professional must begin to view retailing as a key extension of their professional service and an added benefit to their client, as well as the business, rather than as just a part of their job, which will eventually begin to bring satisfaction and enjoyment in the process. It goes without saying that retail sales increase a spa's revenue stream, but in order to boost sales, all members must be aware of how important retail products are to the overall treatment strategy. This entails advising or promoting retail home care products, so that the treatment could continue back home, and the client continues to enjoy that great feeling.

Rather than just looking at selling products, they must start looking at them selling results and it is these results that are at the heart of an organizations future in terms of building long lasting relationships with customers and the profits into the business. When the client takes back homecare products that result in an extension of their treatment at the spa, it adds value to the professional service and allows the benefits to last longer- leading to customer retention and referrals. For this the therapist must be able to convince the client that homecare is just as important as professional treatments, and is key to achieving the desired results.

It starts with the therapist/ beautician believing in the products they sell: The first and most important step in retailing professional beauty care products is to believe in the products yourself

The products you carry in your salon or spa must be products that you are also using on your customers. When they see how beautiful they are after using "the product" they are prime for suggestive selling. You need not be pushy. A simple *"you can duplicate this texture and softness of your hair by using product X".* Show them the bottle after you apply it to their part and ask, "doesn't this smell like xxxx, wait till you see the results"!

When to Retail? The fastest approach to selling goods and services is by recommendation, and the ideal time to make a recommendation is while a client is seated in front of you. Instead of doing this at the conclusion as most people believe, retailing actually begins when the client is still in front of you, undergoing the therapy. There is no better person to know about the client's condition than the person doing the treatment. Therefore, immediately following or during a treatment, it is crucial for the professional to explain to the client the suggested, prescribed at-home regimen. The expert can explain throughout the treatment how good homecare will strengthen and prolong the positive effects of this professional experience. The topic of your chat should be how you can make their lives easier while also assisting them in feeling and looking beautiful. How therefore can we encourage current customers to utilize your services more frequently? Bring it up with them! This essential action must however, never be left to the receptionist.

During a treatment, clients are practically in the hands of the skin/ hair/ body care specialist, relying on a deep level of trust. So as a therapist/ specialist, make sure you carry that trust into a sale at the end of every treatment for a profitable transaction which is mutually beneficial. When selling in a spa environment, there is a strong and intimate impact. For example with a doctor's appointment, you wouldn't expect to leave without a prescription after the doctor examines you. So also, to achieve the best outcome, the treatment of your client must be continued with the required home-care recommended by you!

While retailing, it is important to make a reference to a product covered in the therapy, which can be a very successful link to sales, as customers have already experienced and tasted this first hand and therefore will be more confident about this recommendation that you are making for home-care.

The key to integrating selling is the intimacy and time a customer and expert share together. As an expert, after a treatment, of around say an hour, you have literally touched the patient for around an hour, if not more and this helps increase the bonding and trust. So do all you can to live up to this trust that you are building on.

Most times it's a good idea to provide free consultations as a springboard for retail purchases and upcoming treatment reservations. Even if the client does not immediately book a service, a consultation may pave the way for a significant on-the-spot retail transaction and the development of new client relationships. The secret to retail sales is knowledge and first-rate customer service that should go above and beyond what the customers expect each time they come in. After receiving treatment, no expert should ever allow a patient to leave on their own and head for the door. The skin/ hair care specialist/ beautician/ therapist or whoever the expert is must meet the customer at the point of purchase to close the sale by describing and reconfirming the recommended products, ideally using a customized prescription sheet. This may also be the perfect time for the professional to recommend the next visit and offer a rebooking incentive.

Get them to Sample: At any point during the appointment, stop the conversation and mention the product you're using. Explain that you're going to put it onto a small section of body and ask the client to feel the difference it has made. Once the client is happy that the product has made their body /hair look and feel better, or more manageable, ask whether they'd like you to use the product all over. It then becomes much easier to tell the client about the product; that is if they haven't already asked you.

Customers enjoy trying things before making a purchase. After a consultation, providing samples is a terrific approach to foster trust and give customers the impression that they are in a pressure-free setting. At the conclusion of a sale, samples of products recommended should be provided so that customers can test them, as customers become more at ease, confident, and prepared to make the buy when they have the opportunity to feel, touch, smell, and experience a product. Offer free samples of products that provide instant gratification and produce results after one use, such as a makeup primer or cooling eye gel

What to Retail? As spa/ salon owners you should be cautious to look at what selective products to retail and not overwhelm clients with too many options. It is also important for the products you sell to be in sync with your philosophy and the services you offer. Are your treatments mainly preventive, restorative, or corrective? Juggling too many product lines can create confusion.

A-Answer Customer's Concerns and Objections

An important component at this stage (or can happen earlier too) is: The Handling of Customer Concerns or Objections. During the Sales Process, even the best salespeople can encounter objections that are difficult to handle. However if you have followed the GREAT Sales Model, the chances are that they would be genuine concerns and to a minimum.

An objection is a concern or question raised by the client that delays or prevents you from proceeding to the next step. By using the right techniques, however, you can handle these objections without losing your focus.

Whenever I come to this part I am always reminded of why farmers place a 'scare- crow' in the middle of a paddy or rice field. The answer is obvious- to scare away the birds. But a clever bird knows that behind this so called 'scare-crow' are juicy grains- or his food! So also, I believe, that a smart sales person knows that behind every objection there is a genuine need to buy! The objection in question must however be handled or cleared before progress is made.

Why do you think customers raise objections?

During the sales process customers will raise objections for many reasons. At some stage, customers could:

- ✓ *Misunderstand something you have said.*
- ✓ *Feel pressurized.*
- ✓ *Are not convinced about your claims.*
- ✓ *Haven't yet made up their mind.*
- ✓ *Have to go back and justify their buying decision to others.*

One of the most common times objections are raised is just <u>before</u> the decision to purchase. Just before making a buying decision the buyer worries about making a mistake. Every time someone decides to pull out his/ her wallet there is always a question and hesitation that runs in their mind*: 'Am I making a right decision'* and is therefore often looking for reassurance that the decision to buy is the right one.
We must understand therefore, that objections form a natural part of the buying process. And we all do this every day, even for the smallest purchase, so why get worked up when the customer does so?
So if an objection is raised at this stage, it means that the buyer has an unanswered question or concern that the expert has to deal with and it could most times be a positive rather than a negative situation when a customer raises an objection

Broadly, there are basically **two types** of objections that you will encounter:
Doubt
Indifference
Doubt, sometimes is referred to as distrust, and is expressed when the customer doesn't believe something you have said.
Indifference on the other hand is expressed when the customer feels that what you have said is not important to him/her- the customer may simply feel that it is not appropriate to their situation.
Both types of objections occur for specific reasons. To overcome an objection, you need to recognize why it occurred and then deal with it, **immediately.**
Clarifying Objections
Clarify what the objection is (express empathy if appropriate)

Then respond accordingly:

To remove doubt:

- ✓ *Refer to a similar situation and/or*
- ✓ *Offer evidence or proof that what you have said is true*

To handle indifference:

- ✓ *If based on a misunderstanding or lack of information, explain your point more thoroughly*
  And/or
- ✓ *Outweigh the indifference with the benefits of your suggested approach*

Now we need to deal with the objection: Once you fully understand the nature of the objection then it can be answered in different ways depending on whether it is

- ✓ A misunderstanding by the customer
- ✓ Disbelief over claims you are making
- ✓ A product disadvantage.

You will now need to verify that the objection is removed or cleared from the mind of the customer and to ensure it does not come up later. Your next step would be to 'advance the sale'.

The key to objection handling is to react less quickly when an objection is raised and find out more about the problem. Clarify exactly what the problem is; then try to overcome the objection. Finally, if you have dealt with the objection successfully and it is the right time, close the sale, or move on to the next stage of the sales process.

EXERCISE: *Before we go any further, list down all the possible objections you have come across so far or you come across regularly* (Whatever comes to your mind): We would get to dealing with them as we move forward.

Most objections or customer concerns can broadly be classified under **4 key heads**, as you will see in the illustration.

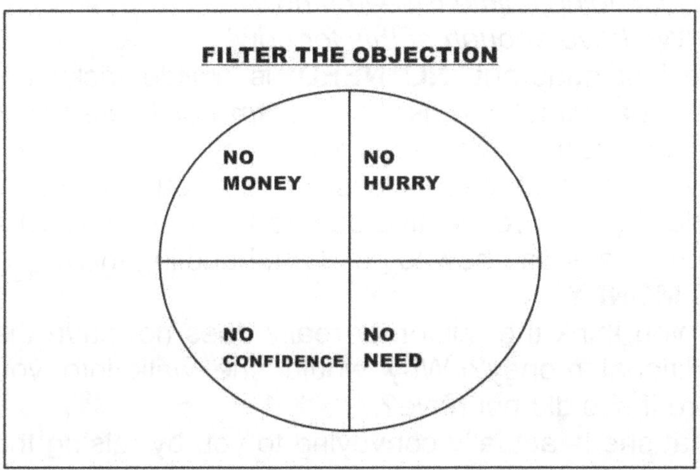

Now try to classify under which quadrant each of your objections (you listed above in the Exercise) fall in under:
For example; if a customer says: *'Your prices are too high'* or *'You guys are very costly'*
Obviously this would feature under the quadrant **'NO MONEY'**
Another example for 'NO MONEY': *'I need a discount!'*

'I don't want to deal with your company again. I had a bad experience last year'!
Or *'Never heard of this brand…not too sure about them'!*

Examples like the two above will fall in under the '**NO CONFIDENCE**' Quadrant.

An example of what would come under the quadrant of '**NO HURRY**' would be something like this: *'I am fairly happy with what we have now. We could possibly look at this later only'*

'My daughter's birthday is coming up in September. I am just doing a little research now"

Or *'We have enough of this for now'*

The last quadrant '**NO NEED**' is a little tricky and could be something like this: '*I am not interested in this'* or *'I don't think you guys can help'*

Now once you have classified all your objections under the four respective quadrants, let us see what each means and how to go about handling them.

NO MONEY

Do you think the customer really does not have that additional money? Why would she walk into your store if she did not have?

What she is actually conveying to you by raising that concern that falls in this quadrant is that she does not really see value in your proposition. And most times it will be that the expert has been rattling off features of his/her product or service, without really proving value of how the customer will benefit or what it would do for her.

TIP: Keep 'FAB' in mind. Prove value by translating the relevant features to benefits. What is in it for the customer? What will it do for her- translate into tangible benefits that she can see, that far outweighs what she would be investing in.

NO CONFIDENCE

There could be 2 scenarios here:

1. A past customer who has had bad experience and now no more wants to deal with you

2. A new customer who has never heard of you and doubts your company's capability

If it is a past customer, how would we go about building her confidence again in your company and service?

TIP: Talk to them and show them testimonials of satisfied customers-pictures/ videos or arrange to provide the telephone numbers of such customers, case stories of how you resolved similar cases and the outcome, have them connect on phone right away with such customers who will talk well of you etc. You could also build on the USP's of your company, particularly relevant to their need

If it is a new customer, who has never heard of your company and doubts its capability, then how would we go about instilling and building her confidence in your company and service?

TIP: This is where the USP's prepared under the step 'E'- will help. You could highlight the USP's of your company particularly relevant to him/her and their need. Show them testimonials/ video clips of satisfied customers, etc. Particularly of interest would be your credibility, standing in the market, your after-sales-support and financial status. What can you demonstrate to prove this?

NO HURRY

How do we get the customer to move forward or commit on a decision now?

TIP: Look at what incentives you have now that the customer could benefit by.

What if your company does not have the required material or product when they require?

With the costs of raw materials, labor etc going up, what is the guarantee that he/she would get this same product/ service at this same price?

NO NEED

Any objection falling in this quadrant is probably one of the most difficult. There are 2 possibilities:

1. There is genuinely no need- She may not be a likely customer
2. She has a need but has not disclosed it

If it is the second scenario, then we will need to go back to step 2 of the GREAT Sales Model which is asking Revealing Questions to uncover further. If the customer is still unwilling to reveal, then in most times it could be something personal about you as an individual that she is put off with.

TIP: Take their telephone or contact details; allow a few days for her to cool down, and then have someone else from your organization call them to build up again, inviting them to your store- with maybe a free consultation or free one-time offer.

Handling the PRICE Objection

Price is probably one of the most common objections we hear in sales. Customers will say *'you are too expensive'*, but before we react, we need to think about what it might mean when they say so.

Sadly, most sales people respond immediately with a *'No Sir/ Madam....'* rather than trying to understand what was in the customers mind when she said this!

You need to put yourself in the customer's shoes!

Perceptions Differ! We need to specifically understand...

How short is short!

How firm is firm!

How slim is slim!

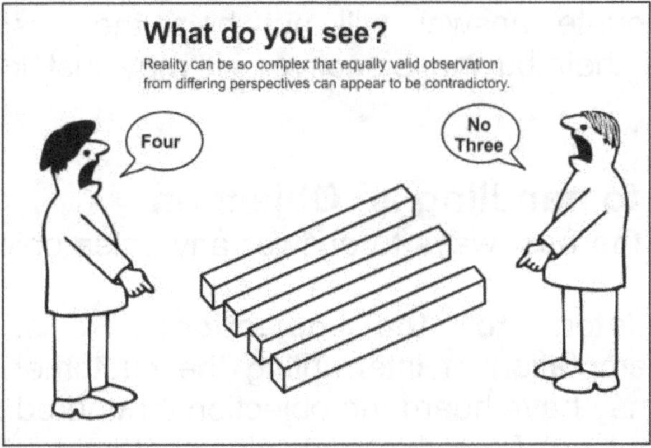

As seen from the 2 illustrations above, perceptions of individuals differ. So all the more it makes sense to clarify the customers understanding of *'prices are high'* or *'too expensive*' before we hastily jump into handling the same

Too expensive could mean several of these and more:

- ✓ *I've had another quote/ offer*
- ✓ *I'm checking you out*
- ✓ *I'm negotiating with you*
- ✓ *I have to go back and convince others*
- ✓ *It's more than I expected*
- ✓ *It's more than I have in my budget*
- ✓ *I don't want to buy from you*

This is why it is so important to clarify this objection before we attempt to handle it. We need to find out the real reasons behind the objection. Often we react too quickly and give what we feel is the right answer, but in fact we could be totally wrong.

The customer may have had another quote and may have constituents to satisfy. They may be looking for help etc. Interrupting or not clarifying but giving an inappropriate answer will not help the customer achieve their buying objectives- it may just kill the sale!

Steps to handling an Objection

One of the best ways to answer any sales objection is to:

1. **Listen to the objection:** Resist the temptation of interrupting the customer. You may have heard the objection a hundred times but not from this particular customer. It may also be that the customer has more than one objection, or that this particular objection is slightly different than the ones you usually hear.
2. **Empathize**: This means that we express our understanding of our customer's perspective

in words: *"I understand how you feel; this is a large investment."*

When a customer objects to something, she is handing us her problem... and is waiting for us to start overcoming the objection... In most cases that's what we do. The problem is that the customer may not be ready to accept our solution. Empathizing with her therefore will help create a state of mental readiness.

Few 'do's' to keep in mind when empathizing and clarifying customer's objections:

- ✓ *Do listen. Don't assume*
- ✓ *Do ensure our tone conveys true empathy*
- ✓ *Do be patient*
- ✓ *Do pause before responding-Don't rush the answer*

3. **Ask for clarification**, by restating the objection in our own words to ensure that we have correctly understood what her actual objection is: *"Do you mind if I ask you why you feel that way?"* or *"So what you're saying is that you don't see the value in this, is that right?"*
4. **Prevent further objections arising:** Actually one great way to ensure that this objection never surfaces again or another one does not come up again after you've handled the first one is to ask a question that could go something like this: *'Mr Customer, before I go into answering this concern for you...let me clarify...Is this the only concern that is preventing you from moving forward?"*

   In most case the customer will say *'Oh, Yes'*. Now what you've actually done is to indirectly prevent her from coming up with any further excuses in the future!

5. **Filter the Objection**: See which of the 4 quadrants of NO MONEY, NO HURRY, NO CONFIDENCE, NO NEED (covered above) it falls into
6. **Seek permission:** This is also known as 'bridging'. We are asking the customer for permission to provide a solution. By taking this approach, the customer will be much more receptive to our feedback, first, because we asked for permission and second, because she gave the permission, with the advantages and benefits being that it will reduce the customers hostility, we will earn more trust, we will thoroughly get to understand the objection, which will give us additional time to formulate a response. *"Would it be ok if I explained some of the benefits of having this?"*
7. **Provide a solution:** Explain a solution that best suits her need
8. **If Price, clarify the objection:** To clarify the objection you could say something like: *"When you say we are expensive, could you be a little more specific, Ms. Customer?"*
   Listen to what the customer says. She would then clarify why she feels you are expensive. Based on her answer you could move forward. If she is comparing you with the competition, then use your differentiators to stand out.

EXERCISE: ***What are your most common objections you face? List them. Then using the steps provided above, how would you go about handling each of them.***

T- Techniques to help customer's 'buy'…as people hate being sold!

"We need to earn the right to ask our customers for their money"

If you have come up to here, then you are now at the fifth and final step of the GREAT Sales Model, and as you will realize this particular step is a mere formality of wrapping up the entire discussion and working on the add-ons.

This may follow soon after you have answered and cleared your customer concerns and objections with some customers (for example to new customers) or can happen immediately after step three with other customers that have already dealt with your company (who are familiar with the features and benefits you have to offer and your brand/ company)

It is the process of now presenting your specific product or service solution to fulfill one or more needs identified during step two of the model, along with complementary add-ons.

Steps

- ✓ Summarize the client's needs(s)/desires/ problem(s)
- ✓ Recap the Value from your product/ service related to the need(s)/problem(s)
- ✓ Recommend the appropriate Solution
- ✓ Obtain the client's commitment to take the action that you have suggested or recommended.
- ✓ Introduce the complementary add-ons

Before we go into suggesting complementary items/ add-ons we need to touch on one key

point at this stage: What prevents people from closing?

Many sales people are looking for 'closing techniques' that will make the decision making process easier and take away some of the pressure felt by both buyer and seller at that moment of truth, when a decision is about to be made.

The problem is that at this point the sales person is worried about getting rejected and how he/she will have to face the boss, whilst the buyer is worried about making a mistake. So it is all too easy for either or both sides to delay the buying decision, rather than risking rejection, or taking the wrong decision

It is up to you as the expert to have the confidence, at the right time, to ask for a commitment and risk rejection. That is your role and unfortunately, 7 times out of 10 sales people fail to ask for this commitment and this can make them lose the sale they have worked on so far to achieve- by allowing the customer to move away to a competitor/ elsewhere. All your hard work is eaten up by the competition.

Research has shown that 70% of sales contacts end up with the salesperson not asking for a commitment, as fear of rejection takes over and they miss the opportunity to close. While many sales people see closing as being about techniques this is not actually the main issue.

Closing is about **timing** rather than **techniques**.

So what then is 'Closing'?

The sales process is about seeking out problems/issues/needs/desires and trying to identify solutions. We cannot close the customer, or gain some sort of commitment from them until there is an identified need for our solution.

It used to be said in the earlier days '**ABC of Selling'**- meaning to "**A**lways **be c**losing" but this approach does not fit in with a relationship style selling that is long term. The right time to close is when the customer is ready to buy. If the sales person is always trying to close this will irritate most customers and they will probably reject the salesperson- this is also one of the reasons why this is the most hated profession. So closing is about timing, not technique. The best way to sell is to make it easy for the customer to buy. The close is important and we should have the confidence to ask for the order at the appropriate time. However, we must put the close into perspective and keep selling simple.

Watch out for Buying Signals

A smart sales person will be alert to watch out for certain 'buying signals or clues' that customers can give you to let you know they are interested and ready: Effective Observation and keen listening skills can help!

- ✓ The customer comes in with an advertisement, either from you or your competitor.
- ✓ She goes directly to the item she wishes to buy.
- ✓ Her eyes light up when you present and discuss the product.
- ✓ She involuntarily reaches to try it on
- ✓ She asks for time to discuss it.
- ✓ She asks questions about style/ packs/treatments etc- options.

- ✓ She shows excitement. She becomes more animated. (Pay close attention to the facial expressions)
- ✓ She talks about the products using words denoting ownership. ('I'll use my pack…)
- ✓ She makes positive statements about the product.
- ✓ She says, "I'll take it."
- ✓ She now asks about payment methods or options, especially for higher priced products
- ✓ She starts to talk about how she will use the product at home- denoting ownership already
- ✓ She talks of using the item on a particular occasion
- ✓ She makes positive statements about the product and continuously keeps agreeing with you with a knowing smile.

The goal here is to keenly watch for a combination of buying signals without making it obvious- the more signals are emitted, the stronger the desire and the need for you to close.

EXERCISE- Buying Signals: ***What are some other buying signals that you have encountered- work on listing the various Buying Signals that you need to be ready for….***

Moving the situation forward when the client shows interest

A client will indicate that she agrees with your recommendations in several ways. She may:

- ✓ Book an appointment for the recommended treatments
- ✓ Purchase the recommended products

- ✓ Book a consultation with the other recommended consultant
- ✓ Order the delivery of the product if not in stock
- ✓ Pay an advance amount towards a course of treatments
- ✓ Buy a gift voucher to give as a present.
- ✓ Asks for a membership form

It is important at this stage, when the customer is really eager, for you as the expert to just **shut up!** (I have seen many sales personnel messing up at this stage by opening their mouths on something irrelevant and allowing the customer to go off on a tangent- thereby delaying or postponing and sometimes even losing the sale all together!)

Selling to the Opposite Sex

Research suggests that women and men have different sets of criteria and are opposite poles when it comes to shopping or making a purchase.

Men see shopping only as a necessity, while women enjoy it as an experience. You can see this happening as men will usually walk in and out of an outlet, most times in a hurry; while women will often casually take their own time to browse the entire outlet.

Men will pick up items that are needed and head straight to the check-out, billing counter- Men are usually not comparison shoppers. But women will walk up and down, maybe several times, read labels, compare brands and explore options. Men tend to focus on their logical needs when making a purchase

- ✓ *Does this product have this feature?*
- ✓ *Will it be able to do…?*
- ✓ *Does it have the feature I am looking for?*

For men to feel confident in your outlet, you will need to be well versed on male skin conditions and knowledge on the best products for treating them. Using masculine colors will appeal to men. Address issues that are of concern to men- like appearances, looking for ways to combat signs of aging, or want to manage certain skin conditions, relax, or de-stress? Men value discretion and like to have their privacy respected. Men are loyal to product brands and prefer a friendly sales approach. Men are usually not comfortable asking questions, until they become quite comfortable with the salesperson and tend to move through the decision making process quickly and logically in their minds:

- ✓ *Does this product meet the needs?*
- ✓ *Will it solve my problem?*
- ✓ *Is it what I am looking for-features, price etc?*

Women on the other hand, most times operate with emotional needs when making a buying decision, and will focus on how the item will fit them/ their looks/ their lifestyle…how will it make them feel.

You as the sales person/ beautician would need to therefore ask a lot of open-ended questions, to make her feel comfortable and demonstrate that you care:

- ✓ *"Tell me more about your desire for …"*
- ✓ *"How was your experience at…?"*

Women will tend to give out more information than men, but be cautious when closing with her, for if she is pushed into making a decision too quickly, it may backfire. Women want to be listened to and know that they have really been heard, wanting to have their concerns taken seriously and want answers to their questions immediately.

They enjoy detailed information about products or services, taking time to process things. So they want their time to be respected.

When dealing with women, trust is a big factor in developing relationships with women. Giving them what they want before they ask for it will help you to win their loyalty. And remember that most times women value a personal referral from a trusted source

When Men Sell to Women

- ✓ Focus on establishing a relationship with her, by looking in the eye
- ✓ Soften the initial moments by asking; *"Is there something in particular you're looking for?"*
- ✓ Instead of jumping in to discuss the product, invest time to learn about her needs
- ✓ Ask open-ended questions and start by asking permission to do so: *'Would you mind if I ask you a few questions?'*
- ✓ Concentrate on listening and talking less
- ✓ Periodically paraphrase to fully understand her needs
- ✓ A good way to begin the presentation would be: *"Based on what you told me…"* This will prevent her from thinking you are giving her advice
- ✓ Incorporate people/ testimonials/ customer feedback into your presentation as most women love to hear of other people
- ✓ Avoid jargon and technical terms-use feelings, words and emotions to describe the product
- ✓ Avoid getting into 'one-upmanship'
- ✓ Ask, "*What would you like to do next?*" rather than jumping into an aggressive close.

Selling to Teenagers

Teenagers are one of the spa clientele groups that is expanding the quickest and a big segment to watch for-but not all spas are set up or ready to serve them yet. To cater to this segment, it helps to have a thorough understanding of teens' behaviors and psycho-social requirements if you choose to market to them.

Few points to keep in mind when dealing with teenagers: Teenagers of today are much smarter, brand and tech savvy, and highly media-driven. They are also highly influenced and impacted by their peers and the pressures that come from it, resulting in them being more interested in goods and services that will improve their appearance/ how they look in front of others- the new fads and trends.

When delivering a service or treatment on them, remember that they prefer multitasking; messaging, texting or watching videos on the phone.

Teenagers' skin care needs are unique. So study/ examine teen publications' that cover more of skin care, makeup, hairstyles, and fashion trends. What services do they prefer, the trends in such as spa parties, makeup applications, manicures and pedicures, waxing and hair styling?

As teenagers have a tendency to speak their minds out loud, especially while travelling in groups, this could be a big disturbance to others in the salon/spa areas. So you might like to consider creating a separate area only for teens if you have the room and want to promote to them.

Generating Additional Sales: Suggesting Complementary/ Add-on Products- Up-Selling/ Cross-Selling

Cross selling and up-selling are crucial to increasing every sale. You are maximizing your per-customer sales, by giving your customers more value for their money. Studies indicate that acquiring a new customer is 5 to 25 times more expensive than keeping a current one, so working on up-selling and cross-selling is a far more profitable way to grow a business with your existing customers. Up-selling and cross-selling is a wonderful opportunity to get ahead of your competitors and increase the value of your customers, while ensuring that you meet your revenue goals in a way that profits your business the most. Both cross-selling and up-selling are opportunities to provide addition to what the customer has already intended to purchase.

What is most important to keep in mind is being ethical by ensuring that the ultimate need of the customer is foremost. Remember: Never recommend an up-sell or cross-sell where if it isn't necessary.

Up-selling and cross-selling are often used interchangeably, but they are actually two separate entities. As a professional, you will need to understand the specific differences between the two and what they mean for the customer and how they can help customers if you are to implement them.

The most world-wide well-known example that is used over and over again in trainings to indicate the distinction between up-selling and cross-selling is McDonald's. The waiter is spontaneous when he asks you: *"Can I make it a Supersize?"* which is a typical example of up-sell, while *"Would you like some fries with that?"* is a cross-sell example. The counter sales person will always ask if the customer likes something else: desert, salads, or ice cream. And imagine, these are just teenagers that do that!

The first example is that of adding up to the product, while the other is offering a completely different, but complementary product. The first case is when you help a customer decide to buy a little extra, an add-on or up-grade, while cross-selling is when another service or product is sold.

Up-selling and cross-selling are really just a matter of offering something else your customer is likely to want, based on what they are already buying now.

The examples mentioned here, simply and elegantly illustrate the point of up-selling and cross-selling, while the sales person has effectively offered the customer additional value, ensuring extra revenue for the establishment...and off course, in this example, even a higher tip. These are usually small purchases that the buyer doesn't have to put a lot of thought into and would not really mind adding on. The bonus is they can be extremely profitable for you and for your organization.

How does up-selling and cross-selling help your business and customer?

- ✓ Increases Profits: It's a fabulous opportunity for additional money. Growth does not mean just retaining your customer; it also means that you also look at opportunities to grow the revenue from each current customer.
- ✓ Helps Increase in ROI: You have already carried out the hard work of marketing, finding and selling successfully to your customer; which is indeed a costly affair. Therefore if you now neglect to up-sell and cross-sell, it would be like throwing away additional money that is

otherwise yours. Up-selling and cross-selling to your customers will allow you to see a profit quickly and receive a better return on your investment.

- ✓ It Increases Customer's Loyalty: When you up-sell and cross-sell, you are indicating to your customers all the options in front of them, so that they could make knowledgeable choices and decisions, thereby conveying to your customers that you care for them, which results in trust and loyalty. And delighted customers are your best form of advertising that you cannot otherwise buy.
- ✓ It increases Customer's Lifetime Value: Not only will up-selling or cross-selling bring in a greater initial profit after signing on the customer, but the overall value of the customer over the course of their lifetime will also be greater. Not only will you increase their lifetime value by increasing the amount they buy over a period of time, but by increasing their loyalty, you will see much more from a customer that stays loyal to you. Again, the increase in customer loyalty will pay off over the long run.
- ✓ Your Customers enjoy Convenience and Flexibility: Many customers do not want to shop around for a new avenue when they need a certain product or service. By offering them more choices or relevant add-ons, they do not have to take a risk with a new company to get what they need. Most customers will stay with what they like if they know what is available. Since you have established trust with the customer, you can have the first

opportunity of their business by offering them the related products and services you offer.

Important issues to keep in mind when up-selling and cross-selling

- ✓ Know in advance what products/ services can be paired/ clubbed. As a professional, you should already have fore-knowledge of the broad selection of complementary or additional services/ products in your head, before a customer ever walks into the salon. When a customer makes a purchase from one category, you should already be thinking about up-selling all the complementary categories and add-ons for that item.
- ✓ Determine which products get the best results for each customer
- ✓ Make it relevant. Although up-selling and cross-selling can be great tools for the customers, sometimes it can be annoying for the customer when the recommended add-ons do not relate to them or their experiences. Relevance is key in up-selling and cross-selling. It goes back to knowing your customer, and keeping track of their needs to ensure that you are making relevant recommendations that will enhance your relationship. Offer up-sells and cross-sells that make sense.
- ✓ Demonstrate value before making the pitch. Focus more on the emotional side of the decision.
- ✓ Work at being a sales consultant for customers: Become an expert in what your customer needs. This way, instead of

simply trying to "sell" a service/ product to a potential client, you can suggest ways that other services/ products can serve/help your customer. Find places that they could improve by using your product or service. You are in the perfect place to make suggestions because you are a product expert and have insights to offer that they can't find elsewhere. This expert understanding can make you come across as a professional consultant versus just a salesman.

- ✓ Be proactive. Many people make the mistake of assuming that the customer will ask for specific accessories-this is not always the case. Take the time to understand early in the consulting process what issues and problems your client might have that you can utilize to solve. Don't wait for your customer to ask about an additional item or upgrade. They don't know about solutions or upgrades unless you tell them. Instead, brainstorm for your client and come up with solutions for their possible problems for them.
- ✓ Always offer one up-sell/ add-on offer at a time
- ✓ Showcase your products. Complementary items and add-ons should be prominently displayed at eye level and reach, as it makes it easier to cross sell to customers from a display when they can clearly visualize how the item works together. Related items should be kept near each other. You will lose out much if you have to

walk to another end of the store only to find an item to match the one you have.

- ✓ There is no limit to accessorizing. All it takes is initiative, creativity and your imagination!
- ✓ Trust is vital: Customer relationships are all about trust and this comes from getting to know their wants and needs. When you come to understand your customer, you can easily anticipate their needs and offer them the products and services right for them. Customers trust will always ensure you earn a more expanded business.
- ✓ Up-sell and cross-sell with integrity.
- ✓ Pick the appropriate time – there are always times when it is not appropriate to up-sell, like when your customer rushes in and wants to quickly rush out- She is in a hurry!
- ✓ Use this opportunity as a way of getting some feedback- if they don't take the add-ons, ask the reason. Is the offer not strong enough; is it a budget issue or simply a limit to how many of products a person may need?
- ✓ Track the customer journey: It is important to keep track of all of your customers purchase/services availed, so that you will get to know more of their likings, desires, preferences and all purchasing interactions. An integrated CRM will let your company to both understand the specific customer and allow anyone to both cross-sell and add to the customer journey.

- ✓ Reward customers for their loyalty: When a customer takes an additional step with you to spend more and remain loyal, take the initiative and reward them for it, by showing your thanks and this could include something small, like sending them a thank-you letter or offering them a free gift or discount code for their next purchase

Effective strategies to maximize your sales

- ✓ Assumptive is the key: You've got to assume that the customer will naturally want this. Begin the add-on with a brief benefit, then, if possible, add something unique about what you are selling. What is the value they are going to derive from this? How will it help them?
- ✓ To avoid sounding pushy, particularly if the up-sell requires some elaboration, ask for the customer's permission to describe it.
- ✓ Get customer involved. Always enable a 'hands on demonstration'! One of the most effective add-on techniques is getting the customer to use the product right there in your location. For example, you might like to put some 'Facial Cream' into the customer's hand and show her how to apply it herself.
- ✓ By showing the client how to really experience the product in a live setting, you are creating a value-added up-sell.
- ✓ The consultation always provides a good opening to talk through alternative options to the client's normal treatments, For example: *'I know that you have booked in for an eyebrow tidy with tweezers next week. But did you*

know that an eyebrow wax is great for giving a clean finish to the shape and lasts a long time?'

"I notice your skin is fairly dry on your feet. How about a pedicure and warm paraffin treatment to soften and moisturise the skin? We have a special offer going on at the moment.'

- ✓ The next time a customer is re-booking her regular facial why not say something like, *"To boost the treatment results of your Classical Facial I can offer… (*the up-sell you can offer). *While still offering you the wonderful relaxation of the Classical Facial it has the added benefits of…* (describe the benefits)*".*
- ✓ What has to be relevant is that the up-sell must suit the customer's skin care needs this will empower the therapist to up-sell effectively and with integrity.
- ✓ By providing the link to additional treatments you are not introducing lots of different options all at once. The client will in fact be pleased that you are taking such an interest and will not view it as an intrusion or a hard selling approach
- ✓ Encourage up-selling and cross-selling opportunities by promoting add-ons with gifts to purchases.
- ✓ Set up advertising displays in high-traffic locations to create hotspots, and maintain best-sellers and travel-size items in the checkout area to stimulate impulse purchases.
- ✓ Once a month, choose a staff favorite item and highlight it with a beautician or therapists' image and quote to make it special, individual,

and relatable. Even a small token gift is always appreciated by customers after they make a purchase. It might truly brighten their day. You might like to consider offering various levels of gifts based on the customer's purchase amounts. If a free present is being offered with a purchase, advertise it at the front desk or on a door or window. Create signage's that highlight specials in the lobby, treatment rooms, and check-out area. This will assist bring in new business, and if customers are aware that they frequently receive a small gift or sample with a purchase, this incentive will keep them faithful and bringing their business only to the spa.

More on Up-Selling and Add-ons

As seen, up-selling salon or spa services/ products not only increases sales but just as importantly it adds value to your customer relationships. An example would be to suggest an additional service that complements one in which the client is already interested, offer a higher quality product, or sell additional supplies, such as spatulas and sponges to be used with products.

For example if a customer is just having the same routine waxing service each time she comes in wouldn't it be beneficial to her if she could have the hair removed on a more permanent bases with IPL or Laser. If the answer is yes and these options haven't been recommended then this is another lost sales opportunity. Potential profits could be walking out the door every single day. Can your salon spa business afford this to be happening?

The best part of up-selling is that it's practically effortless. Since it's done after the customer has decided to go ahead with a major purchase on a service, the hard part of the sales conversation has already been done. It is simply about persuading your customers to take more from you. Let's say, they want to buy one of your products…What about taking 2 or 3? Or they want to avail of your services for a year…What about committing to 18 months instead? Or give them a package or bundle of services rather than just the one thing that they normally take.

Up-selling is just presenting the information in a "by-the-way" assumptive manner. You're doing your clients and customers a HUGE disservice if you don't tell them you have something else they may want or need. And you're leaving money on the table in your own business.

Here is an example of related products and services that can be looked at when cross-selling/ targeting add-ons:

For a Facial treatment, the other services could be:

- ✓ Steam treatment
- ✓ Electrical facial
- ✓ Eyebrow shaping
- ✓ Eyelash tint
- ✓ Make-over
- ✓ Make-up coaching lesson
- ✓ Products for home-use

Here are a few examples of Add-ons

- ✓ Upgrade the quick conditioner to a deep conditioner for just XXX more. Add the paraffin treatment to the manicure for only XXX.

- ✓ Do a nail art item with every manicure for a special price. Upgrade to a French manicure with hand massage for only XXX more.
- ✓ Combine a mini facial with your massage for just XXX and it only takes an extra 15 minutes. The options and opportunities are endless.

They just need to be easy, uncomplicated, and provide a true value for the extra few bucks.

It is also recommended for the spa team to have a customized "prompt sheet" of all services and products that complement, support and add benefits to all treatments on the menu. This would aid therapists to upgrade their guests' experience with targeted add-ons or products, for example, by offering special masks or serums during a facial treatment or up selling a muscle-relaxing gel or roll-on to guests suffering from muscle aches and pain

EXERCISE- Cross-sell

Product/ Service	**Other Products to cross-sell**

EXERCISE- Up-sell

Product/ Service	**Other Services to up-sell**

Always Look at Rebooking Clients

Upon checkout, satisfaction should be confirmed, and if there is any negative feedback, address it immediately. Offering to book an additional appointment and a thank you by name is essential.

Some clients are just forgetful or lazy when it comes to rebooking an appointment. If you haven't seen a client in four-five weeks, send out a message reminding them to book their next appointment. If they still don't after that, you could even lure them with a discount voucher or an add-on service. Since they belong to the lax segment, you must make it easy for them to book by including a link in your message to your online booking page on your website

Tips for Re-booking

- ✓ See their Pre-history
- ✓ Their trend once every 3 months
- ✓ Their usual day and time- could be a pattern (say Tue/ Wed@ 5pm)
- ✓ Show customer, block and confirm

Finally, the experience of completing a sale, whatever is the size usually gives every sales person a joyous feeling and the word **'SALE'** says it all:

***S** - **S**uch*
A** - **A
***L** - **L**ovely*
***E** - **E**xperience!*

The Importance and Benefits of Providing a GREAT Experience

We are beginning with this subject, because if we get this right- we have all else falling in place. This is the KEY!

No business today can afford to ignore two very important people: 2C's –Your Customer and Your Competitor! The person in front of you is your Customer, and if this person is not treated well, then the person behind you (Your Competitor!) is just waiting to grab her as she drops from your list!

Therefore knowing how to win and retain customers is the single most important business skill that anyone can learn. The business world makes way for the person who brings in the business and the money…and that's the person who wins and keeps customers.

In today's service-oriented economy, great service is more than a competitive weapon-it's a survival skill but distressingly only a few organizations are really delighting their customers. Rest assured that if you don't provide this great service, someone else would! This therefore has to be the key focus of every organization: to remind themselves that every single person in the organization from the topmost person, whether, the owner, director or manager, right to the lowest in rank can effect or have an impact on customers, by the way they treat them and therefore must have the 'hat' of a customer service professional always on. Sales and Service are not to be looked at as separate functions-They are two sides of the same coin, both having the same ultimate goal- To satisfy the customer! In today's world it's even more important, where Sales, Marketing, Service and Operations share a common goal: Creating and Retaining Customers. And to create and retain customers we have to combine Great Selling with Great Service.

So what then is this **Great Sales and Service Experience**?
Customer Service or their Experience is the customers' perception of how your outlet treats them. These perceptions affect their behaviors and build memories and feelings that will drive their loyalty. In other words: if they like you and continue to like you, they are going to do business with you and will recommend you to others. And for your customers to like you, you should know them very well to create and deliver personalized experiences that will entice their loyalty. But gaining this in-depth knowledge about customers isn't something that just happens. Spas, salons, health clubs will need to work on this with their customers. No doubt, this is well worth the effort.
And it doesn't matter what kind of business you are in – improving the experience for your customers is the key to increasing retention, satisfaction and sales.
Here are some vital data that can help open your eyes to this area of your job on priority

- ✓ *For consumers, customer experience will become more important than price and product after 2021.*

- ✓ *89% of businesses compete through the level of customer experience they're able to deliver.* -Gartner
- ✓ *70% of the customer's journey is dictated by how the customer 'feels' they are being treated.* -McKinsey
- ✓ *Businesses that deliver better customer experiences obtain revenues between 4% and 8% above their market.* -Bain & Company
- ✓ *55% of customers are willing to spend more money with a company that guarantees them a satisfying experience.* -Think Jar
- ✓ *70% of unhappy customers whose problems are resolved are willing to shop with a business again*. -Glance
- ✓ *Customer service statistics show that new customers cost anywhere between 5 and 25 times more than retaining existing customers.* -Harvard Business Review
- ✓ *44% of consumers take their business elsewhere due to a poor experience.* -NewVoiceMedia
- ✓ *50% of customers switch brands when their needs are not met.*
- ✓ *13% of customers tell 15 people or more if they have a negative experience.* -Esteban Kolsky
- ✓ *After one negative experience, 51% of customers will never do business with that company again.* -NewVoiceMedia
- ✓ *72% of customers will tell 6 people or more if they have a satisfying experience*. - Esteban Kolsky

- ✓ *67% of customers report a bad customer experience as the reason for switching businesses.* -Esteban Kolsky
- ✓ *Only 1 in 26 customers will tell a business about their negative experience; the rest simply leave according to customer service facts.* -Esteban Kolsky
- ✓ *79% of customers who share their complaints online see their complaints ignored.* -RightNow

And here are some more reasons why customer care is important. These were highlighted in a survey carried out by the CBI (Confederation of British Industry)

- ✓ *Only 1 customer in 26 with grounds for complaint actually does so.*
- ✓ *Those customers who experience problems tell between 8 and 15 people about the problems.*
- ✓ *9 out of 10 people who complain and have a problem that is not dealt with satisfactorily will never buy again from that supplier.*
- ✓ *9 out of 10 people who complain and have a problem that is dealt with satisfactorily will buy again or come back.*
- ✓ *It costs 5 times more to attract a new customer than to keep an existing one.*

Customers usually don't care about what good you do! On an average when a customer is happy with a product or service, they would generally tell an average of around 7 people, but if the service was bad or if they were disappointed with it, guess how many they would tell on an average?

Without considering the internet, the answer is an average of 38 (just lip service)! But today, with everyone in possession of a mobile phone that has an internet connection, you do not have to guess the figure!
Bad News certainly travels faster than Good News! You don't have to look far...See today's newspaper headlines, or turn to any news channel or get onto any social media site or platform...What do you get more of? Good news or bad news?
Word-of-mouth advertising is therefore the most powerful form of advertising in the world. And this is what you as a Professional need to keep in mind!

Remember- there are only 3 entrances to your business; or for that matter, to any business....

- ✓ *The Front Door!*
- ✓ *The Telephone!*
- ✓ *The Internet!*

...And if either of these are NOT handled well, you have LOST your Customer forever!
And in some businesses, this figure can be very high. And in this business which is more of women, remember women can be great INFLUENCERS!
A typical business hears from only 4% of its dissatisfied customers. The other 96% just quietly go away and 91% will never come back. Now that can be a serious financial loss for companies whose people don't know how to treat customers, but a fabulous gain to those that do!
The average business spends six times more to attract new customers than it does to keep old ones. Yet customer loyalty is in most cases worth 10 times the price of a single purchase/ sitting. As markets become increasingly competitive,

customers can now immediately go elsewhere if they don't get what they want- in fact they can do so from the very comfort of their bedrooms- by calling on services to their homes. Continuous overall improvement, gaining competitive edge, increasing market share, raising profits- None of these things is possible, unless businesses can find new ways of maintaining the loyalty of customers.

So what then are the benefits of providing Great Sales and Service?

Great service will always enable your business to:

- ✓ Spend lesser on advertising-Word of mouth works!
- ✓ Differentiate itself from the competition
- ✓ Improve its image in the eyes of the customer and stakeholders
- ✓ Minimize price sensitivity
- ✓ Improve profitability
- ✓ Increase customer satisfaction and retention
- ✓ Build a database of committed customers
- ✓ Have a number of advocates or evangelists for your company who will talk well of you.
- ✓ Enhance its reputation
- ✓ Ensure products and services are delivered right the very first time
- ✓ Improve staff morale
- ✓ Increase employee satisfaction and retention
- ✓ Encourage employee participation
- ✓ Improve and increase productivity and performance
- ✓ Reduce costs
- ✓ Create a reputation for being a caring, customer-oriented company
- ✓ Build on a list of responsive suppliers

- ✓ Foster internal customer/supplier relationships
- ✓ Work on bringing about continuous improvements to the operation of the company
- ✓ Focus on an improved management team
- ✓ Have safer and insured future

EXERCISE: ***Now try and tailor this to your outlet/organization's need by thinking of all the benefits to You, Your Team and Your Organization by providing 'Great Sales and Customer Service'***

And remember, delivering 'Great Sales and Customer Service' that makes a positive, lasting impression on customers, takes more than courtesy…it's much more! It starts with understanding that Great Sales and Customer Service is from the customer's point of view. Many organizations spend a lot of time looking inwards and are organized accordingly. The truly customer-centered organization takes time to think through the procedures and systems that work best for the customer. This puts the customer at the very center of the organization.

How Customers are lost!

In a single year…Millions of customers are lost because of poor service!
Customers are LOST
Referrals are LOST
Repeat business is LOST
And…Guess who wins?
Your COMPETITION!

And who do you think are the culprits…
ALL OF US!
We are all unknowingly contributing to these statistics?
"I am new to this salon"
"It's not our policy to…"
"It's not my job…I handle something else"
"You're not the first to complain about this"
"Sorry you've come to the wrong department"
"I don't see what the problem is…"
"You've come at the wrong time"
"I can't do that…"
"It's over there…"
"We don't have that"
"I'm busy right now"
"You will have to wait..."

Here's how we could define bad service in the context of this business.

- ✓ Unfriendly staff
- ✓ Unhelpful staff
- ✓ Poor knowledge of products and services
- ✓ Not enough staff around to assist
- ✓ Lack of choice

- ✓ Complicated/ difficult returns procedure
- ✓ Items not within reach/ difficult to locate products
- ✓ Lack of cleanliness and hygiene
- ✓ Therapists/ beauticians- not focused, wasting time

Some ways to give your customer's a bad experience…

- ✓ Being constantly engaged
- ✓ Did not greet or acknowledge the customer
- ✓ Passing them from department to department/ or person to person
- ✓ Did not try to understand their need, but delivered a rehearsed presentation and began the service
- ✓ Did not handle the customer's concerns/ objections
- ✓ Making them repeat their story each time you transfer them
- ✓ Having them on hold forever, without periodically checking up
- ✓ Treating them as a 'nobody'
- ✓ Telling them that it's not you're your job/ fault/ policy/ problem
- ✓ Bluntly telling that the item is out of stock
- ✓ Not providing them satisfactory solutions but just 'passing the buck'
- ✓ Forgetting to do what you said you would do
- ✓ Your tomorrow never comes- Commitments are never kept

A survey on **"Why customers quit"** found the following:

- ✓ 3% move away

- ✓ 5% develop other friendships
- ✓ 9% leave for competitive reasons
- ✓ 14% are dissatisfied with the service/ product
- ✓ *68% quit because of an **attitude of indifference** towards the customer by the owner, manager or some employee.*

(With the total showing 99%, you could be wondering what happened to that 1%- Well, because of the death of some of them!)

If you do a little calculation, you will find that a well over 90% is all within your control of turning this around for your organization. Studies show that increasing customer retention rates by just 5% will increase profits anywhere from 25% to 95%, depending on the business you are in.

Improving customer retention is essential to growing spa sales and the overall profit. It is cheaper to retain existing customers than acquiring new ones, and the success rate of selling services to them is much higher. They become your advertisements. In this industry, studies reveal that while the probability of selling to a new customer is only 5% to 20%, the probability of selling to an existing customer averages 60% to 70%. Therefore, just 20% of the existing customer base can generate up to 80% of future spa profits.

And remember that your customers won't love you if you give poor service, but your competitors will certainly love you!

Most of the examples cited above on why customers are LOST, have a lot to do only with the human side of dealings. In other words when a customer is disappointed with their expectation of this side (the human behavior) of the service, they CHANGE the service provider without even complaining! The figure below illustrates this well:

Your Customer's Experience

The overall encounter by your customers, that mostly depends on the various 'moments of truth' they experience and the consequences as a result!

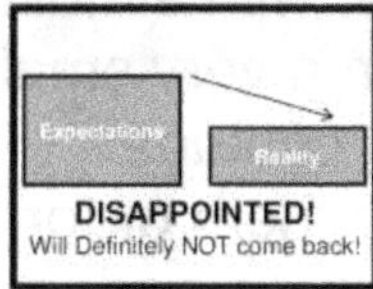

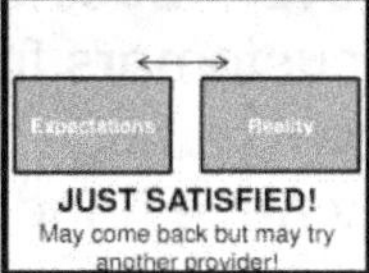

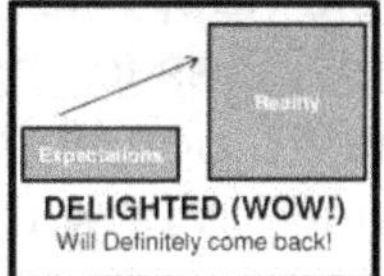

The Customer Cycle

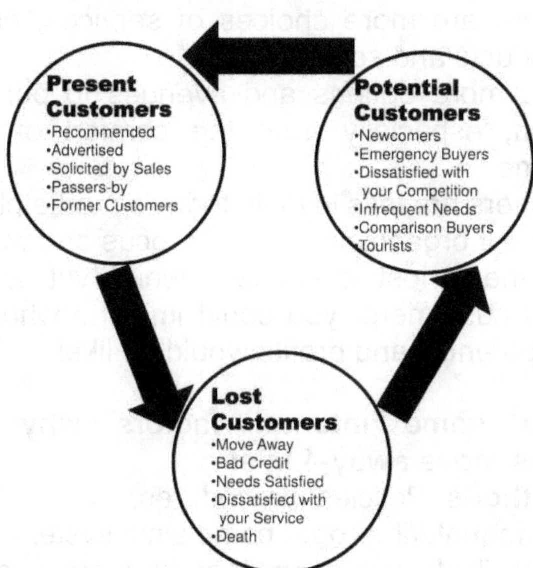

An Understanding of the Customer Cycle

The figure shows the typical customer cycle and the 3 groups in a market:

- ✓ The Known Market or Your Present Customers,
- ✓ The Unknown Market or Your Potential Customers,
- ✓ The Lost Customers!

This cycle happens in every business, with almost every business losing customers from a very small fraction of a percentage to a huge percentage, depending on how they have handled them or for other reasons. As fast as a customer is gained, one or more is lost!

…Moreover markets and customers are constantly changing

- ✓ Competition is greater than ever.
- ✓ There are more choices of services, outlets, products and services
- ✓ And more options and avenues to purchase from, especially from the comfort of one's home

So, customers are less loyal in today's marketplace

But imagine if organizations are to focus and work on retaining these lost customers while yet winning those new customers- you could imagine what their business potential and profits would be like!

Here are some internal factors why your customers move away-4 M's!

- ✓ **Methods**: Policies/ procedures, inadequate/improper complaints system, lack of flexibility, values unclear, hierarchies etc
- ✓ **Materials:** Documentation- too much paperwork, outdated information, website,

apps outdated/ not updated, outdated technology

- ✓ **Machine**: Less treatment machinery, equipment/ billing machines/ equipment to handle customers/ queries etc
- ✓ **Men/Women**: Employees demoralized, little or no training, poor attitudes etc

EXERCISE: ***Now list all possible reasons how your outlet/ organization could be losing customers due to <u>Internal</u> as well as <u>External</u> Factors and what you/ your team could do to prevent this situation from occurring in future***

How valuable are Customers and what do they really want

Knowing how to win and retain customers is the "SINGLE MOST" important business skill that anyone can learn!
The business world makes way for the person who brings the business and money through the door...the person who wins and retains customers!

Don't underestimate the value of a single customer!
Think for a moment and consider just how valuable customers are. A customer alone makes it possible for you to earn your livelihood in the way you do! If those customers stop coming in, your establishment will not have its business to keep and pay you and its other employees. Just one customer can make or break an organization, depending on how they are served or treated. Today with the internet in the palm of every person's hand, there is enough bad-mouthing that can be done in a matter of minutes-that can ruin an organizations image and credibility in no time!
The average business spends six times more to attract new customers than it does to keep old ones. Studies have shown that increasing customer retention by just 5% can have a bottom line profit increase of up to 75%. And the 'Lifetime Value' of a single customer can be measured in many millions, depending on the type of business.
Therefore every customer must be considered both as a powerful tool for word-of-mouth advertising as well as an appreciating asset. Just compare these

two: When you build or buy machinery it starts depreciating the very day it is ready. But the well-serviced customer, on the other hand, is an appreciating asset. Every small act on her or his behalf zooms up the chances for repeat business, add-on business and priceless word-of-mouth referral.

What do customers want? Customers buy experiences!

This starts with their very first contact with you…on phone, person or the internet!

And remember- as we've seen earlier, there are only 3 entrances to any business….

The Front Door!

The Telephone!

The Internet!

…And if either of these is NOT handled well, you have LOST your Customer forever!

What do your Customers want?

Various researches have identified a number of factors that seem to influence customers' decision to remain loyal.

- ✓ You keep your commitments/ promises
- ✓ You demonstrate your willingness to help: you display a genuine desire to do so
- ✓ You and your entire organization inspire confidence
- ✓ You treat customers as individuals (All five fingers are not the same!)
- ✓ You make it easy for customers to do business with you.(Are you open/ available when they need you; have you tried calling your own telephone lines to see if it is easy

getting through; have you tried setting up someone to act as a 'mystery customer' to see how your outlet treats them)

- ✓ All the physical aspects of your outlet, services or products give a favorable impression (parking lots, toilets, billing counters, display racks, lighting, music, temperature, ambience etc)

Know what your customer's want!
All callers want C.A.S.H.

Convenience (at theirs, not yours!)
Action (not just lip service!)
Speed (Everyone wants an answer immediately/ early/ now!)
Hassle-free (Not being shunted from one person to another!)

When it comes to making a purchase, 64% of people find customer experience more important than price.

Other Factors:
Convenience-

- ✓ Convenient at their time
- ✓ Available help, Efficient service
- ✓ Items at their reach
- ✓ Delivery as promised
- ✓ Phone/internet support
- ✓ Hassle-free returns
- ✓ Quick resolution of problems

Great People-

- ✓ Friendly, helpful, courteous, empathetic, trustworthy, sincere/ knowledgeable, accurate

- ✓ Able to anticipate needs and recommend solutions
- ✓ Appropriate appearance and demeanor/ attitude

Only 'GREAT' Customer Service gets noticed

- ✓ Are your customers delighted with your service and do they want to come back to you?
- ✓ Can they be easily enticed by a competitor that makes an extra effort to satisfy them?

Great Service is about…

- ✓ Treating Customers with respect and thinking of them as people the organization might be able to help with its services and products, rather than just 'someone' to be dumped stuff
- ✓ Learning what each customer needs, and going beyond what customer expects
- ✓ Being supportive and offering help after the service/ sale, and not rejecting requests for help once the money is in
- ✓ Developing life-time relationships with customers and not just wanting to make a quick sale
- ✓ Demonstrating personal credibility (Adding value and integrity to each interaction)
- ✓ Discovering new ways to 'delight' those who you serve

EXERCISE: ***From your experience of handling customers in your outlet/organisation, what do you think your customers want or expect from you/ your team/ organization?***

Handling Complaints and Irate Customers

What if, every time a customer complained, you looked at it as if a **'Complaint is a Gift',** rather than extra work or them being a 'pain in the neck' to you?
Unfortunately, what often happens is that the front line employees who receive complaints take them personally or blame others. As a result, they over-react and become defensive.
To overcome this kind of reaction, it can help to think of the complaint as a gift- as a genuine desire to solve the problem by someone who has taken the time and the trouble to visit, write or telephone.
It is a chance to set things right! And probably, the only chance! That is why it is like a gift- The customer has given you another opportunity to rectify/ change things. And if you don't change, He will change! (by moving to your competition!)
How many times you would have noticed that all that the customer really wanted when she complained was an acknowledgement of the problem, an apology, an explanation or a solution to the problem…And most times the solution offered could have been just a hearing out!

By complaining, customers are giving you several opportunities like:

- ✓ Helping you find out what you need to do to improve your systems and procedures
- ✓ See your service from the customer's point of view and try to make changes- He is the spokesperson for the many others that do not open up.

- ✓ Identify areas where your company could train your staff.
- ✓ Help you identify new products/ services/ opportunities which the market may require from you. (This is free information that you can get!)
- ✓ When customers share their story, they're not just sharing pain points. They're actually teaching you how to make your product, service, and business better.

So what do customers look for when they complain?

A customer who has taken the trouble to complain to an organization expects:

- ✓ **Someone to listen** actively to the complaint, to be sympathetic and to take responsibility for its resolution
- ✓ To **deal** with **one or two** people only- not to be shunted from person to person or department to department.
- ✓ And a **quick** solution.

By encouraging your customers to complain, you help resolve their problems quickly and effectively:

- ✓ You keep existing customers
- ✓ You develop your relationships with them.
- ✓ Those customers are likely to win you more customers because they will go and tell friends and relatives how impressed they were with you.
- ✓ The original complaint itself becomes unimportant!
- ✓ You now have another brand ambassador

But…why most customers do not complain?

Here are several reasons that might sound familiar to what could be happening in your organization:

- ✓ *I tried complaining in the past- but nothing really happened*
- ✓ *I don't think anyone will listen to me- they seemed to be only after my money*
- ✓ *Nobody is willing to take responsibility over my complaint- but just keep passing me from one person to another*
- ✓ *I don't think my complaint will be welcome*
- ✓ *Whenever I make a complaint, I am looked at and treated with suspicion and doubt- always treating me like a criminal and subjected to interrogation*
- ✓ *I am not treated politely. They are very rude when I complain, but treat me on top of the world when getting my business*
- ✓ *I don't know who or how to go about complaining- no access provided on their website or elsewhere*
- ✓ *If I send a complaint in writing, it takes so long if they do reply, but most times they never even get back.*
- ✓ *Complaining is more trouble than going elsewhere*
- ✓ *Their websites and other promotional material talk so much of how customer focused they seem, but all this is only in empty words- they really don't mean it!*

What are some of the Key Pre-requisites for handling complaints?

- ✓ Top Management to have the 'Right Attitude' (as this attitude very soon percolates down-knowing what is done, is what the organization rewards)

- ✓ The 'Right Attitude' and Behavior of people receiving and handling the complaint
- ✓ Strong Systems, Policies and Procedures-friendly and fast (Not just smiles!)

What if you put yourself in your customer's shoes?

You cannot truly understand your customer's experience or how your customer feels without putting yourself in his shoes. Learn to deploy empathy and awareness to the other person's needs. Knowing your customer's wants and needs is one thing. Understanding "the why" behind their decisions is another. Try asking yourself-If the same incident happened to you:

- ✓ *What would your initial reaction be?*
- ✓ *What would you think and feel? Why?*
- ✓ *What questions do they have right now that would really clarify the problem we solve, and a need for its solution?*
- ✓ *What would you expect from the service provider as being fair to you?*
- ✓ *What would I most want in the long run by solving the problem?*
- ✓ *What would it require to make you happy-to continue to be dealing with the service provider, by being their 'goodwill' representative and talking only well of them*

By putting yourself in your customer's shoes it will help you understand the customer's needs and expectations and place you in a better position to be able to handle the complaint efficiently

Here are a few 'Golden Rules' for processing complaints:

- ✓ Always thank the customer, explaining why you appreciate the complaint raised
- ✓ Apologize for the mistake/ error/ slipup/ behavior etc
- ✓ Take ownership to resolve the problem
- ✓ Commit to do something about it immediately
- ✓ Verify that your proposed solution will address their needs
- ✓ Work on correcting/ rectifying the mistake/ error immediately
- ✓ Check to see for the customer's satisfaction
- ✓ Work on putting a system in place to prevent such mistakes from occurring in future

Handling Complaints requires RESPONSIBILITY!

- ✓ Where errors/ mistakes/ slipups have occurred, resist the urge to argue, to defend, justify or to provide excuses
- ✓ Admit mistakes and apologize sincerely- you are the representative of everybody in the organization- you are the brand ambassador.
- ✓ Even if the request or the problem sounds familiar, don't jump to conclusions until you have gathered all the facts
- ✓ Offer to follow-up personally; give your name and number. Customers want consistency in their dealings with the company, and prefer not to explain their situation again and again to someone new.
- ✓ Look for solutions, not obstacles or excuses!

A few DON'TS to keep in mind!

- ✓ Do not appear disinterested.

- ✓ Do not lose your temper or show your exasperate on with the situation to the customer.
- ✓ Do not let the customer know this is as common a complaint if you have heard the complaint many times before.
- ✓ Do not appear inflexible. Saying, *"well, it's company policy', or, 'We can't do that'*, will aggravate the customer.
- ✓ Do not blame other people. The customer is not interested in your internal politics; he or she needs a solution to his problem now.
- ✓ Don't get defensive or argue about complaints. Be empathetic.
- ✓ Don't make the customer repeat their complaint. If you have to transfer their complaint, either in person or on the phone, show the customer you have been listening by summarizing the problem for your colleague.
- ✓ Don't leave the customers waiting in the office or holding on the phone too long. Keep them informed. Offer to call back if you don't have the information.
- ✓ Never tell them what you can't do for them. Emphasize what you **can** do.

Key steps to handling complaints:

- ✓ **Thank the customer:** The fact that the customer has come or called to complain, means that they are giving your organization a chance to rectify things. You have another opportunity to turn this customer as a well-wisher. She could have gone away quietly- but she has given your organization another chance- grab it and use it to turn the customer around.

- ✓ **Listen and stay calm**: Aim to diffuse the customer's feelings and clarify the exact nature of the problem.
- ✓ **Don't justify, argue, make excuses, interrupt or pass the buck**: Just stick to the facts, keep off what happened in the past and focus on what is going to happen now.
- ✓ **Sympathize:** This means sympathizing with the fact that the person has a problem, not accepting any blame as you are currently hearing only one side of the story (theirs).
- ✓ **Ask probing questions to verify facts:** This will give you more detailed information about the specific complaint and allow you to see a way through to a possible solution to the problem
- ✓ **Check back your understanding:** Reconfirm or paraphrase what you heard.
- ✓ **Agree a course of action and timeframe**: It is essential to find a solution which is satisfactory for the customer and from your organization's point of view.
- ✓ **Check that the course of action is carried out:** If you agree with the customer that something will happen by a certain date, you must check that it has in fact happened. If it hasn't, you must take action to avoid making the problem even more serious.
- ✓ **Check for the satisfaction of the customer**
- ✓ **Thank the customer**
- ✓ **Work on setting your system** in order to ensure such mistakes or lapses are not repeated

Delight your customers, while resolving complaints!

You choice of words are to be 'POSITIVE' to demonstrate empathy!

- ✓ Never say: *"I don't know"* (Instead say, *"That's a good question, Let me just find out for you"*, or offer to get back, after finding the answer…')
- ✓ Never say: "I/we can't do that" (Instead use positive statements, such as, *"This is what I/we can do."*)
- ✓ Never say: *"You will have to"* (Instead say, *"you may need to"*, or *"I need you to please.."* or *"Here's how we can help you"*)
- ✓ Instead of *"Sorry to keep you waiting"* you could say, *"Thank you for waiting/holding"*.

Turn Negative to Positive!
Some useful phrases you can use:

- ✓ *"I'll be glad to…"*
- ✓ *"What would you consider right or fair?"*
- ✓ *"I'm sorry you feel that way"*
- ✓ *"Would you be willing to…?"*
- ✓ *"Thank you for drawing this to my attention."*

Dealing with IRATE Customers

What sort of Customers do you honestly like or prefer?

'Nice Customers' (the ones that do not shout or get agitated)

or

The 'Barking' Ones' (the emotional/ irate ones)?

Most people love these so called 'nice customers'- the ones that do not shout, and avoid the 'barking one'. But it's these so called 'nice customers' that are dangerous- they will slip away to your competition, without even telling you.

The so called 'barking ones' are those that are giving you another chance to change- grab this opportunity. And these few are the representatives or spokespeople of the many that are slipping away, without providing you any feedback. So welcome them with open arms!

How to deal with IRATE Customers

- ✓ Give the customer space to let off steam before you try to steer them towards a discussion
- ✓ Don't take it personally, and always be calm
- ✓ If the customer is abusive and you can't steer the conversation onto how you can solve the problem, seek help from your supervisor
- ✓ If the customer won't calm down and they've caught you unprepared, agree to look into the problem and tell them when you'll call or e-mail them

Always remember that: An Angry Customer...May have 4 F's that could be bothering them!

- ✓ **F**itness: They may have a health problem
- ✓ **F**amily: They may have a spouse/ children/ other family problem
- ✓ **F**inance: They may have a money problem
- ✓ **F**irm: They may have a job problem (boss/colleague/ other)

And they may just be taking that out on you!

Take it seriously – <u>not</u> personally.

When handling a highly emotional or irate customer, think of the acronym: **'LEAPS'**

- ✓ **L**isten: Allow the customer to vent out all their feelings. Do not interrupt or argue
- ✓ **E**mpathize: Acknowledge the person's feelings (*'I understand how you feel about this…I would have felt the same too'*)
- ✓ **A**pologize, even if the problem is not your fault (You could say, *'I am really sorry this has happened...'*, and really mean it)
- ✓ **P** (Be) **P**ositive all through the conversation by focusing on the facts and directing your thoughts to your future actions, not the past.
- ✓ **S**olve: Suggest or generate solutions that you can both agree on and/or ask what you can do to help: If reasonable do it/if not, find a compromise.

Steps to handle an Angry Customer

Dealing with an angry customer is an opportunity to learn, and an opportunity to turn a negative situation into a positive customer experience. How you react to an angry customer can make or break the perception the customer has about your organization.

Instead of backing away or avoiding an angry customer, use this opportunity to improve your product or service, and to work on building a better relationship with your customer. This is a great opportunity you have to solidify your relationship.

Here are a few key steps to keep in mind by taking responsibility when dealing with irate or dissatisfied customers – and turning them around to be your mouthpiece and ambassadors for your organization.

- ✓ Listen all the way out. Make sure the customer has told you everything. Don't interrupt.
- ✓ Ask open questions to understand their problem better, and to find out what it will take to help them – the way they want to be helped.
- ✓ Tell them you understand how they feel (This is powerful- try it!)
- ✓ Empathize with them. (Cite a similar incident or tell them that it makes you upset too) Empathy doesn't necessarily mean agreeing with the customer. It means you truly understand how they feel. Comfort them.
- ✓ Maintain a calm tone of voice all through the conversation
- ✓ Use the customer's name in your conversation
- ✓ Agree with them, if at all possible. (Never argue or get angry.)
- ✓ Take notes and confirm back that everything has been covered, and they have said all they want/need to say.
- ✓ Be an ambassador for your company. Tell the customer you will personally handle it
- ✓ Don't blame others or look for a scope goat. Admit you (and or your organization) were wrong and take responsibility for correcting it.
- ✓ Apologize for the problem they're having. Acknowledging the mistake and letting the customer know you're really sorry will go a long way. Be thorough in your apology.
- ✓ Don't pass the buck. *"It's not my job."..."I thought she said this..." "He's not there right now."...* or *"Someone else handles that,"* are responses that are never right or acceptable to the customer.

- ✓ Avoid negative speech- Tell them what you can do, not what you cannot!
- ✓ Don't take it personally- but do take it seriously
- ✓ Respond immediately. When something goes wrong, people want (and expect) it to be fixed immediately. The customer wants it now- not at your time. Don't we all want it that way when we are customers ourselves!
- ✓ Find some common ground other than the problem. (Try to establish some rapport.)
- ✓ If you have the gift for humor, use it if possible. It is a very powerful tool as making people laugh puts them at ease.
- ✓ Work out all possible solutions, communicate, and agree upon the best solution. Give the customer choices if possible.
- ✓ Follow this up by confirming in writing if necessary. Tell them what you plan to do… and DO IT!
- ✓ Make a follow-up call after the situation is resolved. Check to see if they are totally satisfied
- ✓ Get a letter if you can. Resolving a problem in a favorable and positive way strengthens respect, builds character, and establishes a solid base for long-term relationships. Tell the customer you would appreciate a sentence or two about how the situation was resolved.
- ✓ Ask yourself: *"What have I learned, and what can I do to prevent this situation from happening again? Do I need to make any changes? Where?"*

Processing written complaints

Here are a few key points to keep in mind when processing written complaints:

- ✓ The customers complaint should ideally be acknowledged with a personal letter/ phone call immediately
- ✓ Always thank the customer- clearly demonstrating that the customer is important and explaining why you appreciate the complaint that was raised.
- ✓ A recognition of the customer's right to complain
- ✓ An apology for the mistake/ error/ slipup
- ✓ A commitment from your end to do something about it immediately
- ✓ Work on correcting/ rectifying the mistake/ error immediately
- ✓ A final reply sent to the customer on the action taken
- ✓ Check to see for the customer's total satisfaction
- ✓ A copy of letter to concerned department internally to work on putting a system in place to prevent such mistakes from occurring in future

Letters-Complaints: When handling complaints show 'CUSTOMER concern:

- ✓ ***C****oncern for clients*
- ✓ ***U****rgency*
- ✓ ***S****pecific facts*
- ✓ ***T****imetabled actions*
- ✓ ***O****ptions to resolve*
- ✓ ***M****ailed confirmation*
- ✓ ***E****mpathy for them*
- ✓ ***R****espect*

Always use customer's feedback to:

- ✓ Improve overall systems and procedures
- ✓ Eliminate product defects or work on improvisation
- ✓ Improve the attitude and behavior of your customer service personnel and others in touch with customers through training!
- ✓ Focus the organization more on customer's needs
- ✓ Set higher performance standards

Post-sale:
Credibility to Promote Advocacy
The Power of Testimonials and Referrals

After the Sale- What's next?
Promises and Credibility to Promote Advocacy
When you have done all to give the customer that 'WOW', experience, and once the customer has bought, we still cannot take loyalty for granted and assume that they will keep coming back or referring you to others. They have several other options always in front of them- and they have their money to do so, so we have to keep up that delighted experience. We have to continue to make efforts to retain their loyalty, by keeping in touch with these customers- by following up, informing and updating them about trends and events of interest to them that you gathered earlier.

Your Customer's Experience

The overall encounter by your customers, that mostly depends on the various 'moments of truth' they experience and the consequences as a result!

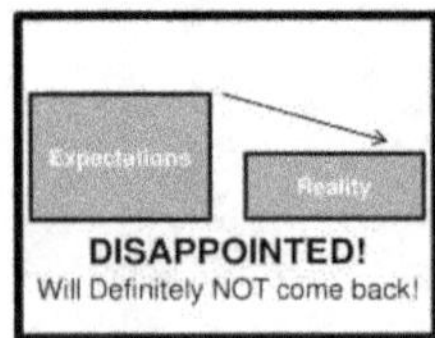

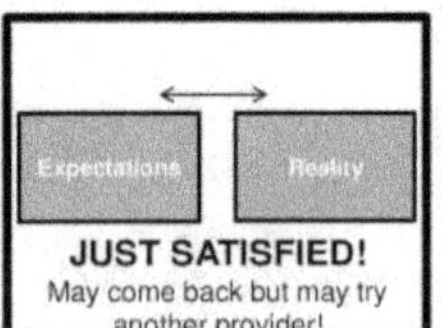

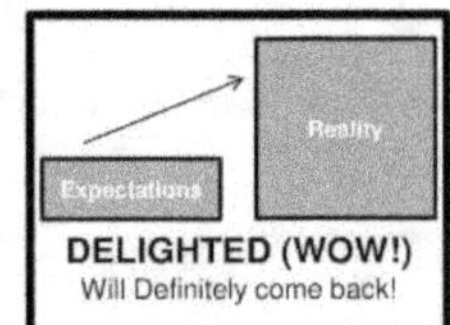

The Sales Follow-up

- ✓ If you really want to stand out from the competition and give people a reason to keep thinking of you, keep in touch after you have finalized the treatment with them
- ✓ When you make the effort to follow up after the sale, it sends your customer the message that you see them as more than a one-time sale
- ✓ Call customers and ask how did they enjoy the experience- do they have any difficulty/ issues that they are facing in using the take-home packs?
- ✓ Send customers a thank you card thanking them for the opportunity to service them
- ✓ Let them know of promotions, sales, events related to their needs or desires that you captured earlier-keep in touch with them-find out what type of communication they prefer
- ✓ Invite them to special events-preferred customer days, product previews/ demos, anniversary mile stones, customer appreciation nights etc
- ✓ Show your gratitude for their trust in you: Once the process is completed, take the time to show your clients how much you appreciate their trust in you. Send handwritten thank you cards or congratulatory notes. The important thing is to show them that you appreciate they chose you over others.
- ✓ Keep in touch at least 4 times each year

Remember, that people want to do business with people they like and trust. As motivational expert and guru Zig Ziglar always says, *"People don't care what you know until they know you care."*

You can only start to build long-term relationships with clients who like you, as people want to do business with people they like. The goal of every professional expert therefore should be to take their prospective customers from *"Lack of awareness"* moving up the other rungs of *learn, like, love* and eventually to the highest form of advocacy and *"Loyalty"*; and to take current customers from *"Like" to "Love" to "Loyalty".*

Therefore a professional expert must be cognizant of the fact that he or she must be liked, but sadly only 40 percent understand and do this. You must work to earn a client's trust and then work to maintain that trust and the most distressing fact is that only 20 percent of professionals actually go this far to complete client advocacy. When you develop client advocacy, you have built a lasting relationship. The client who is your advocate will promote you, recommend you, and return later for additional sales. And you could guess by now what will be the percentage of this category- just two percent of professionals actually build client advocacy. What does an advocate do in a court of law? He will find all means to protect his client from being persecuted or accused. And this is what your client can do if you nurture them to this level or stage. In the customer service ladder in the illustration, this is probably the highest level, where the customer becomes your mouth piece. When you become your clients' star, they'll be more than happy to sing your praises to anyone who'll listen. This business offers the opportunity for almost every client to become a promoter and advocate of your brand. If you treat your customers well and build that strong bond of loyalty with them, there is a good chance they will recommend you to their friends and family when those people have a need for your services.

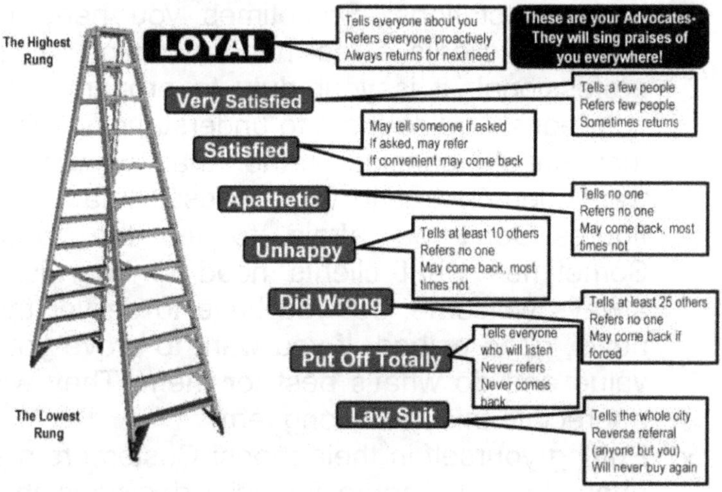

Here are a few things that you could do, to build up and ensure your clients are your advocates or evangelists on your behalf:

- ✓ Professional: These few things are very essential in this profession: Being punctual-responding when you said you would; extremely polite, respectful and courteous; highly prepared, knowing the background and details of clients needs/ your products/ services; listening more and talking less and capturing notes and action points to work on immediately

- ✓ Being Reliable and Responsive: When your clients decide the time has come for a make-do, show yourself to be reliable and responsive to their needs. You don't necessarily need to be available 24/7 but let them know how quickly you will respond.
- ✓ Being honest, and manage client's emotions and expectations: Sometimes you need to give your clients a real honest opinion. As a professional, it is your duty to properly and courteously guide them to understanding what they should consider rather than what they want- demonstrating with necessary fact and figures. Don't be afraid to tell the truth. Sometimes what clients need to hear isn't always welcome, but you have to deliver the news, good or bad, if you want to prove your value and do what's best for them. They will appreciate this in the long term
- ✓ Putting yourself in their shoes: Customers are about to make some financial decisions that they may know very little about, so your role is to help them with their anxiety and be a caring guide.
- ✓ Going the extra mile: Just asking *"Is there something more I can do?"* and going above and beyond what's required is always a winning and a differentiating approach- that will be remembered.
- ✓ Making you and your work stand out. What do you do to set yourself apart from everyone else? Is it your excellent customer service, your likeable personality or your ability to connect with your clients on a personal level? Whatever it is that differentiates you- lean into

your personal brand and use it to provide a memorable experience.

- ✓ Creating tailor-made experiences that are unforgettable: Another thing that can help you stand out is creating tailor-made experiences for your clients. A therapist/ beautician who possesses the ability to anticipate and meet clients' needs, creating a customized experience, positions themselves at the top of the heap. If you can be one step ahead in the process to provide them with a one-of-a-kind, top-notch experience, they'll come back again and again.
- ✓ Staying up-to date and informed: A good advisor has all the facts, and helps clients understand the factors that might impact their decisions
- ✓ Being proactive and anticipating demands: In today's competitive business world, it's critical to keep ahead of the game and improve your company loyalty program strategy to respond quickly to customers' needs.
- ✓ Nurturing past clients: By keeping in touch after a treatment, you're more likely to be the professional they turn to next time and most likely to recommend you to their own network, too. The advantage here is that because you've already got to know them, you will have a wealth of information to keep your communication in line with their requirements. Reach out to them to wish them for their birthday/ anniversary and other special occasions.
- ✓ Being Flexible: The ability to respond positively to changing circumstances, whether

in the clients' situations or in market conditions will help you stand out from the others. Being able to adjust as and when needed is key.

- ✓ Practicing continual improvement. The most successful people never quit improving. Their passion for improvement is acute, and they commit the time, resources, and energy it takes to constantly enhance their skills and performance. No matter how efficient you become, always look for ways to get better. Minor improvements might have beneficial effects on other areas of your work. Remember that the process never ends. To be successful, you've got to dedicate yourself to pursuing quality endlessly. It's not easy, but in these tough competitive times, it's necessary.

Finally, remember that this business is a very competitive profession, therefore it is not enough to just complete the task; you must also display genuine concern and attentiveness to the clients who rely on you -only then, you will be remembered and stand out in this vast jungle

Power of Testimonials

If you've really provided great service, you are likely to receive a host of thankful messages and glowing praises from satisfied clients. But don't just keep them without using these effectively! You can use these as great testimonials and rave about your service for others to note.

Customers are looking for someone that they can fully trust as they decide upon what's probably an important factor in their wellness, beautification and physical and mental state they will be making in their

lives. Human beings by nature will not do business with anyone they perceive to be untrustworthy, and therefore often turn to others, especially people like them with the same challenges, desires and pain points, for advice on the trustworthiness of anything, particularly when it involves their looks, wellness etc.
In key surveys carried out by agencies there has been enough and more evidence to demonstrate the power of online reviews and testimonials in establishing trust:

- ✓ *97% of consumers surveyed searched for a local business online*
- ✓ *73% said positive reviews made them trust local businesses more*
- ✓ *85% of those surveyed said they trust online reviews as much as personal recommendations*
- ✓ *Consumers read an average of seven reviews before they trust and move on to do a business*
- ✓ *Businesses with 10 or more reviews see a 300% increase versus businesses with no reviews.*
- ✓ *And according to Placester.com* 85% of all consumers use reviews to decide on purchases.
- ✓ *They all trust peer recommendations six more times than a normal advertisement.*

Testimonials therefore are powerful trust signals that can go a long way in enticing new clients to your business. They are powerful tools that you/ your organization can use in turning around an unhappy customer or proving the credibility of your service. Client testimonials are just as important as word-of-

mouth recommendations, and they play a vital role in helping you build trust with your potential clients.
Staying engaged and maintaining a good relationship with your clients even after a sale will make it easier to request for reviews, testimonials and referrals. It's best to wait till the client has settled soon after the service before you reach out with a request for a testimonial. If you've never requested a testimonial, it's not too late to start! You can start building your testimonial library by reaching out to clients you've worked with in the last few months and going forward from there, establish a process for collecting feedback and a testimonial from each and every client you serve.
We recommend that therapists/ staff always carry a 'Customer Feedback Book/ Form' with them, and as you reach this stage where you know that the client is elated, then this is the time to bring the book out and have the customer write a few lines on what they felt about you, your service, your attitude, helpfulness etc.
Though testimonials have immense value on your website, you can no doubt use them to attract clients in other ways as well. A testimonial is one of the best gifts you can receive from your clients. Testimonials are words and experiences from past clients and customers sharing their transaction experiences.

How Powerful are Testimonials?
If your service is 5 stars, then the need for you to carry and brag about this is sufficient proof and evidence of who you really are. And who is the best person to say so? Customers who have already experienced your service!

- ✓ Testimonials build credibility and trust: The most obvious and most important reason to add testimonials to your website or keep them in front of you/ your customer is that they build credibility. Obviously, anyone selling their services would say they deliver a great experience; but it's much more believable when we hear it from others who have seen and experienced it firsthand!
- ✓ They have the power to make or break a deal: If they aren't up to standard (or if they are absent altogether) customers will be susceptible to doubt. Salons/ spas without the outspoken support of their past clients are at a massive disadvantage.
- ✓ For some, this is critical for your clients: and is one of the few important decisions in their lives. If something goes wrong, it can have a very distasteful impact on them. No wonder people want to trust the person that does this work.
- ✓ Happy customers are the most valuable advocates for your business: Nothing creates trust as well as testimonials from previous customers who are able to tell that you were professional and trustworthy, and that the entire process went smoothly. Other people are more likely to believe the words of actual customers than what you say in advertisements and other branded content.
- ✓ Draws on emotions quickly: When people who are having similar issues, see their experience and feelings reflected back to them in a testimonial, then reading about that satisfied client's happy ending, allows the potential

client to want to come to you to have the same joyful experience

- ✓ A Good Story is EVERYTHING: Your testimonials should be centered on a good story. By having good characters (past clients), with a problem/issues/ needs/ desires, and how you helped them with their solution (resolution) these stories tap into our brains, pulling us into the plot, wanting more. This is how we relate with the world. And this is why good testimonials draw in your prospects and connect with them emotionally.
- ✓ Customers love being featured: By obtaining a testimonial, not only are you asking for their honest opinion after your treatment is finished, but you're also showing them how much their thoughts matter to you when you post them on your website or show them off to others. In fact most will actually be thrilled to see their words or even photos go live on your website!
- ✓ Requesting testimonials encourages referrals: Having your happy clients write out what they appreciated about your service brings it to the front of their minds and will make it that much easier for them to bring you up when people compliment their gorgeous new looks etc
- ✓ Testimonials can be used long term: Having a bank of strong testimonials boosts marketing efforts and can go a long way as it doesn't matter how old they are.
- ✓ The Process will help you do a self-check and grow: Because this business is so emotionally-charged, you might not therefore always result in a noteworthy conversation, but sometimes clients are itching to share

praise and constructive criticism, as not everyone will be prepared to give a beautiful testimonial, but the opportunity to hear your clients' reflections and sift through them for actionable and helpful criticisms is a gift and a helpful tool in itself.

- ✓ Testimonials helps boost SEO: Adding testimonials to your website can help ensure it ranks high when searches are carried out on the internet.

Remember that your customer's testimonials are much more effective than your own content and advertisements and in order to obtain such testimonials, you need to provide unmatched customer service so that your clients are willing to recommend you.

So how do you get them?

- ✓ Be Worthy of Praise: The first and most important rule to getting testimonials is to be worth it. You can't expect your customers to tell how much they trust you and how well the treatment/procedure/ process went off if that is not true and the best way to find out if your customers are happy is to ask for feedback. If the feedback is positive, then you have a great chance that they would be willing to give a testimonial and do it right away
- ✓ Ask: If you do not ask, you do not get- it is as simple as that. And it is best done face-to-face- as sending an email or message may have them forgetting about it or wanting to do it later
- ✓ Choose the medium: Testimonials can come in different forms: written, audio or video,

- ✓ Questions to ask: *"If you've been happy with my service would you like to give me few lines on what you felt about it"* or *"How would you describe the process and experience with me/ our team?"*
- ✓ Make it quick and easy: Most people do not like spending time writing, especially a testimonial. This is why we recommend carrying a 'Customer Feedback Book' or sheets of 'Customer Feedback Forms' so that you could open up the same at the right time and have them quickly jot down a few sentences.
- ✓ Make immediate use of these testimonials: After you have your testimonials you need to use them effectively and featuring these testimonials on your website and social media is a good start as it will help prospective customers that land on your website or any social media page, to see the recommendations from your previous customers.

What should an ideal Client Testimonial include?
Testimonials must cover some of these key elements below:

- ✓ Must have specific information: How did you help the client / how did they feel/ benefit them?
- ✓ Must be authentic: The testimonial must allow the clients genuine thoughts and personality to shine through the testimonial making others get the sense of how unique the experience was. This can include anything from the fact that you helped them decide on a set of

procedures/ treatments that were essential to see them come out of a situation they were experiencing.

- ✓ Must be thorough: This is an essential item - being thorough in the review will allow other consumers to connect with you, knowing precisely what they will get. Thoroughness includes telling future consumers the events leading up to the end, how the process went from start to finish, and everything you did to help them along the way.
- ✓ Must emphasize the benefits: It must convey to the world how amazing it was to work with you and how you made the entire transaction process simple, efficient, pleasant and memorable. How it was such a pleasure to work with you must be said in the review.

Remember: As a Professional in this trade, this is your most powerful tool- So make the best use of every opportunity to your advantage!

How Strong Relationships lead to Referrals

Trust lies at the heart of all relationships, whether professional or personal. When you work in a business that is based on relationships, such as the spa, salon or health club/ gym, it's easy to see why trust-building is so essential to success. Once you've shown customers that you/ your brand can be trusted, they'll refer their friends and family to you. And this word-of-mouth advertising is the best means of advertising. Recommendations made by close friends or relatives most times influence our purchasing decisions. Look at some of these examples:

How often do we ask someone to recommend a good hotel or restaurant in a particular locality?

When someone asks for feedback on where to buy a car or get it repaired, don't we answer based on our personal experiences?

One of the most effective ways to build trust with new clients is by being introduced by a mutually trusted party. Referrals can make a huge difference in your overall sales during a year. Consider the impact of being able to generate just one referral each week. This will work out to 50 new clients each year, even after you take a 2 week vacation. Now imagine if you were to get one per day! The point is that you can earn more money without working additional hours or shifts and without working harder. Your closing ratio will be much higher with these referrals, as you will now enjoy a certain level of trust with these new prospects. You will find yourself dealing with warm leads as opposed to cold ones. People are more likely to trust you, as an advisor whom they hear about from a trustworthy friend, family member, or colleague, and customers will be more likely to accept your feedback, suggestions, and ideas, because one of their friends or relatives has recommended you. Clients' satisfaction is the best proof of your professional qualities. Encourage your past or current satisfied clients to recommend you to others.

You could do this by asking every customer for a referral *"If you've been happy with my service and know of someone else who could benefit, please have him or her give me a call or drop in."* Then hand them your business card.

Though you can do it by simply asking them, it would be much better to motivate your current clients to tell their family and friends about you by offering them an incentive such as exclusive discounts.

Every time a new client walks in, ask them if they were referred by anyone and add this information to the client profile. This can help you send out a thank you note to the referrer.

Positive reviews make users visit your spa/ salon. While you could offer them some loyalty points for leaving a review, you could also entice them with something small as an example-a free nail polish application on their next visit as a gesture of thanks.

Encouraging referrals is a great way to take advantage of word-of-mouth strategy and build trust with prospects without breaking the bank. Referrals will always be the most powerful source of clients, with a great percentage of customers finding you only via a referral. The more referrals you ask for, the more business you will get. Recognize that referrals can generate additional revenue, without you having to work harder.

A Final Word!

Most of the strategies or steps in this book would have given you a very structured approach and some fresh ideas towards retailing and handling a customer professionally by providing them with a GREAT Sales and Service Experience, but they are certainly not a cure-all. Your products, services and most of all the attitude and behavior of everyone in your organization will do most of the work in keeping customers loyal, for there are no shortcuts. Again, there are many books on sales and customer retention strategies, but this one thing is for sure that will be very noticeable- standing out loud and clear in all of them –that there are NO shortcuts.

You will eventually realise that providing a 'GREAT Sales and Service Experience' results in high levels of customer satisfaction leading to long-term `buying' relationships between suppliers and customers, with customers always coming back!

The 6 Most Powerful Words to always remember in Sales

Your words help you build relationships with customers--so choose them carefully

- ✓ Focus on <u>*Benefits*</u>, not features or *specifications*
- ✓ Focus on <u>*Value*</u>, not *price*
- ✓ Focus on <u>*Show*</u>*,* not *learn/ information*
- ✓ Focus on <u>*Emotions*</u>, not *reasons:* Motions play a major role in most purchase decisions. Never lose sight of how potential customers want to feel: Safer, healthier, smarter, more attractive....

- Focus on <u>*You*</u>, not *I:* While you may desperately need to make a sale, only the customer can choose to buy- so always make the process all about the customer. And…Finally
- Focus on the <u>Customer</u>, leave everything else aside!

And this Focus on the customer can come from following the 5 Super S's as a principle in your store:

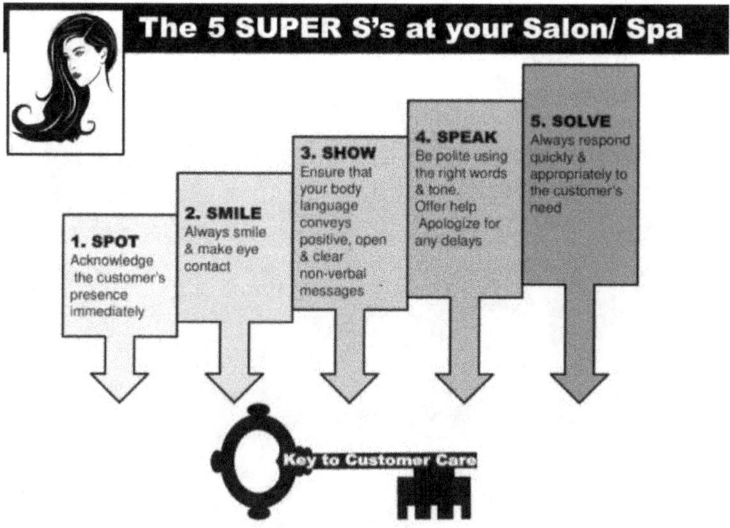

Remember: Your current customer base is the best asset your organization can have. Customers already know your brand, they know your products, and they appreciate your service. So focusing your team's time, efforts and energy on improving the experience for this group as opposed to only being in search of new customers can be a powerful way to skyrocket revenues for your organization.

And here's the **Final Key** that is summed up in one word: **C.A.R.E**:

Customers
Are
Really
Everything!

So go ahead and give your customers that **GREAT** CARE and see your business and profits zoom up!

Get **R**eally **E**xcited **A**bout **T**oday!

About the Author 'GERARD ASSEY'

Gerard Assey is a Graduate in Economics, a PGD in Management (HRD) and holds a Doctorate in Leadership. Gerard holds several International Qualifications in Sales, Debt Collection, Training & Teaching, and is a 'Fellow' of the prestigious 'Institute of Sales & Marketing Management'-UK, a Certified NLP Practitioner, a 'Certified Trainer', an 'Accredited Management Teacher-Behavioral Sciences', a 'Certified Competency Facilitator', a 'Certified Management Consultant'- (the International credentials of a professional management consultant, awarded in accordance with global standards of the ICMCI); and a Certification from the University of Michigan in 'Successful Negotiation: Essential Strategies and Skills'

He is also a Member of the 'National Association of Sales Professionals' backed with several years experience in varied industries, both in India and Overseas. He also holds an 'Etiquette Consultant' Certification from the USA (by Sue Fox, Author of Best Seller: 'Business Etiquette for Dummies'. She has trained some of the top celebrities' world over). He was also a recipient of a scholarship for extensive training in Japan on 'Corporate Management for India'.

Gerard Assey is 'Founder & Chief Corporate Trainer' of the Group: **'Citius, Altius, Fortius Unlimited'**- an organization that **celebrated 20 years of Glorious Service** in 2021, focusing on 3 Core Competencies:

People. Performance. Profit; in functional areas of Sales & Marketing, HR & Organizational Development, covering Recruitment, Training & Consultancy!

Having managed organizations with large Sales Forces in India & Overseas, his specialization cover extensive areas of Sales Training (All levels - Presentation, Negotiation, Key/ Strategic Accounts Management & Managerial Skills for all sectors), Bid Proposal/ Capture Planning/ Management Trainings, Retail Sales, Customer Service & Customer Retention Programs, Training for Prevention & Collection of Debt, Self & Personal Development Programs (Time Management, Teamwork & Team Building, Business Etiquette & Personal Grooming, Leadership & Managerial Skills, People Management Skills, Train-the-Trainer etc), including preparation of Custom-designed Business Manuals for Internal (HR, Induction, and Sales etc) & External use (Instruction, User Manuals).

Gerard has successfully conducted over 5950 Trainings & Workshops (as of May '23) all across India, Middle East, Africa, Europe & S.E. Asia. Besides public programs conducted regularly, both in India & Overseas, he has some of the top names as clients whom he services from Single Owners to large Public & Government undertakings, covering all sectors, for their in-house needs.

His website: www.CollectionSkills.com is the only one in this part of the world to be featured in the 'Collections & Credit Risk Magazine-USA' under 'Who's Who in Training' and ranks TOP, along with other websites listed below on most search engines.

Gerard is author of 61 books already (May 2023),

A few of the business related books being:

1. Bite-sized Bits on Commonsense Management
2. Heart to Heart on Life's Principles'
3. How to become a Successful Manager
4. The Sales Professionals' Master Workbook of S.Y.S.T.E.M.S
5. The Professional Business Email Etiquette Handbook & Guide
6. The Professional Business Video-Conferencing Etiquette Handbook & Guide
7. Professional Presentation Skills
8. Exceptional Customer Service
9. Professional Tele-Marketing Skills
10. Professional Debt Collection Skills
11. The G.R.E.A.T. Sales & Service Workbook
12. Sales Training Advantage for Results (*The Ultimate Sales Training Manual*

    to enable you stand out as a S.T.A.R.)
13. CEO Daily Planner & Organizer
14. The Sales Professionals' Master Daily Planner
15. The Professional Debt Collector's Master Daily Planner
16. My Daily Planner & Organizer
17. MY EMERGENCY INFORMATION RECORD (Family Emergency & Peace of Mind Planner)
18. The Ultimate Therapist & Counselors Planner and Organizer
19. Building an Ethical Workplace
20. Managing Relationships at Work
21. Managing Business Meetings Effectively
22. Effective Delegation Skills
23. Goal Setting for Success
24. B2B Selling by Email
25. Professional Business Etiquette & Grooming
26. Dining Etiquette & Table Manners
27. Effective Networking Skills
28. Grooming, Etiquette & Manners for Teens, Young Adults & Future Leaders
29. Inter-Personal Skills
30. Get Ready, Get Hired!
31. Selling in a Recession
32. Effective Receivables Management in an Economic Downturn!
33. Real Estate & Property Sales Training
34. Credit Sales & Accounts Receivable Management
35. Selling Skills for Real Estate & Property Advisors
36. Take G.R.E.A.T. C.A.R.E!
37. Spa, Salon & Health Club Selling Skills
38. Selling Travel, Holiday & MICE Services
39. Selling Skills for Spa's, Salons & Health Clubs
40. Retailing in Salons & Spas

Besides regularly contributing to business & trade journals, including international ones such as the 'Creative Training Techniques' and the 'Sales News' of the U.S.A, He is also a member of several prestigious bodies & trade associations, having participated in many Conferences & Workshops in India & Overseas.

Prior to his last assignment of leading & managing a large MNC as head, Gerard had a 3-year stint in the Middle East as a Consultant with a leading British Consultancy Firm.

As the past 'Official Country Representative' for the International Business Award- 'THE STEVIES'-(the business world's own Oscar) for about 4 years- he ensured a few Indian companies that qualify for the same every year!

Gerard can be contacted at:

Email: training@Sales-Training.in,training@CollectionSkills.com

Websites:

www.Sales-Training.in
www.EtiquetteWorks.in
www.CollectionSkills.com
www.RetailSalesTraining.in
www.SalesTrainingIndia.com
www.ManualPreparation.com
www.TrainingWithPuppets.com
www.FirstContactAcademy.com
www.SalesAndMarketingRecruiter.com

Our TRAININGS & BOOKS that can help your team

- ✓ **Sales Effectiveness**: Selling Skills for any Sector: Service/ Logistics/ FMCG Realty/ Insurance & Finance/ Media/ SPA's, Health Clubs & Salons/ Key Account Management, Effective Negotiation Skills/ Bid & Proposal Management Skills/ Retail Sales Training: Any Sector (Auto, Jewelry, Clothing, Luxury etc)
- ✓ **Customer Service Skills**-Complaints Handling & Customer Retention
- ✓ **Debt Prevention & Collection Skills**
- ✓ **Etiquette & Grooming**
- ✓ **Leadership & Managerial Skills**
- ✓ **Self & Personal Development Skills**: Presentation Skills/ Effective Communication Skills/Business Proposal Writing Skills/ Problem Solving & Decision Making Skills/ Empowering Secretaries-The perfect PA! (For Secretaries & PA's)/ Effective Time Management/ Teamwork & Teambuilding/ P.R.I.D.E- **P**ersonal **R**esponsibility **I**n **D**elivering **E**xcellence

www.ingramcontent.com/pod-product-compliance
Lightning Source LLC
LaVergne TN
LVHW050546160826
845677LV00011B/2202

* 9 7 8 9 3 9 2 4 9 2 6 2 4 *